PENGUIN BOOKS

CHEKHOV

A BIOGRAPHY

Born in 1900, V. S. Pritchett has had a distinguished career as a novelist, critic, biographer, traveller and, above all, a short-story writer whose mastery of that form is widely acknowledged in this country and abroad. His biographies of Balzac and especially of Turgenev are now followed by a study of Chekhov's life and work.

Sir Victor left school at the age of sixteen to work in the leather trade for four years and later, in Paris, became a shop assistant and then a salesman in the shellac and glue trades while he was learning to write. After four years he turned journalist, first in Ireland after the Treaty, and then in Spain for two years. In 1928 he published his first book, *Marching Spain*, an account of his journey on foot from Badajoz to Vigo, and his first volume of stories, *The Spanish Virgin*. His enthusiasm for Spain resulted years later in the classic *The Spanish Temper*. Since then his stories have poured out in collections: *You Make Your Own Life*, *Sense of Humour*, *When My Girl Comes Home*, *It May Never Happen*, *The Key to My Heart*, *The Camberwell Beauty*, and *On the Edge of the Cliff*, and they have been published in two *Collected Stories* volumes. He has written several novels, notably *Nothing Like Leather*, *Dead Man Leading* (set in South America) and *Mr Beluncle*. His critical essays for Kingsley Martin's *New Statesman*, the *New Yorker* and *The New York Review of Books* have been collected in several volumes, *In My Good Books*, *The Living Novel*, *The Working Novelist*, and in collected volumes, *The Tale Bearers* and *The Myth Makers*. He has written three notable studies of cities: *London Perceived*, *New York Proclaimed* and *Dublin, a portrait*, with the remarkable photographs of Evelyn Hofer. His two volumes of autobiography are *A Cab at the Door* and *Midnight Oil*. He has been International President of PEN and he is President of the Society of Authors. He received the CBE in 1968 and was knighted in 1975. Sir Victor has been awarded honorary degrees from the universities of Leeds, Sussex, Columbia (New York) and Harvard. He and his wife Dorothy, whom he married in 1936, live in London and have a daughter grandchildren.

CHEKHOV

A BIOGRAPHY

V. S. PRITCHETT

PENGUIN BOOKS

PENGUIN BOOKS

Published by the Penguin Group
27 Wrights Lane, London W8 5TZ, England
Viking Penguin Inc., 40 West 23rd Street, New York, New York 10010, USA
Penguin Books Australia Ltd, Ringwood, Victoria, Australia
Penguin Books Canada Ltd, 2801 John Street, Markham, Ontario, Canada L3R 1B4
Penguin Books (NZ) Ltd, 182–190 Wairau Road, Auckland 10, New Zealand

Penguin Books Ltd, Registered Offices: Harmondsworth, Middlesex, England

First published by Hodder and Stoughton 1988
Published in Penguin Books 1990
1 3 5 7 9 10 8 6 4 2

Made and printed in Great Britain by
Richard Clay Ltd, Bungay, Suffolk

To Dorothy

Introduction

I have been an elated reader of all the great Russian novelists and short-story writers since my early twenties and I have often written about them, though I know no Russian and have never been to Russia. The lure for me (I realize now) lay in John Bayley's wonderful phrase—I believe in his learned introduction to Pushkin's *Letters*—that the "doors of the Russian house are wide open": we see people who speak out in the lost hours of the day as it passes through them.

In writing my present biographical and critical study of Chekhov I owe a great debt to the scholarship of others. For Chekhov's stories I have usually followed the remarkable translations of Constance Garnett. They appeared in a haphazard chronology, inaccuracies have been pounced on, but her voice is close to Chekhov's period. I have used her translation of a selection of Chekhov's letters; but I have also turned to the spirited translations done by Avrahm Yarmolinsky and I have learned much from the well-documented translation and extensive notes of Michael Henry Heim and Simon Karlinsky's edition. For Chekhov's biography I have relied on Ernest Simmons's solid volume published in 1962 and rather less on David Magarshack, and on the well-informed commentary of Ronald Hingley, translator and editor of *The Oxford Chekhov*. I have, of course, consulted Prince Mirsky's *History of Russian Literature* and among critics Donald Rayfield's illuminating study *Chekhov: The Evolution of His Art* and its approach to the Symbolists who followed him. I have also read William Gerhardi's lively study written in the twenties. Gerhardi, himself a novelist, had the advantage of having spent his childhood in Russia. There is a rich store of Russian reminiscence of Chekhov in Gorky's memoirs of him, also in Bunin's conversations and in the memoirs of S. S. Koteliansky, who contributed, with Leonard Woolf, a piquant selection from Chekhov's *Notebooks*, published in 1921 by the Hogarth Press. For *The Island: A Journey to Sakhalin* I have used Luba and Michael Terpak's translation, and for *The Shooting Party*, translated by A. E. Chamot, I have used the recent edition with its excellent introduction by Julian Symons. Among selections of Chekhov's works I have also consulted Yarmolinsky's *The Portable Chekhov: The Early Stories 1883–85*, translated by Patrick Miles and Harvey Pitcher; also the *Early Stories*, edited by Nora Gottlieb. For the plays I am indebted to editions by Ronald Hingley and Elisaveta Fen. To all these scholars I owe a great debt.

As a writer and a public-spirited doctor, Chekhov was a restless man, continually working, who refreshed himself by travel. Gregarious though he often was, he was careful to preserve his independence and his puzzling silences. His life story really lies in his work, and his genius, in my opinion, lies above all in his creative gifts as a writer of short stories. I share Ronald Hingley's concern that his supremacy in this genre is nowadays overshadowed by the popularity of his plays with a public that prefers to listen. In fact his plays derive directly from his stories, in which, it seems to me, the texture is far richer. (In the twenties, Prince Mirsky rather coldly said the plays were "infectious, indeed nothing but infectious.") It seems to me that in richness of texture and feeling and the contradictions of human experience, Chekhov is more vigorous and wider in range in master-pieces like *The Peasants* or *In the Ravine*. No play matches *Ward 6* or the leaping imaginative effects of *Gusev* or the anthemlike *The Bishop*. For this reason I have examined the stories in detail and have tried to show the growth of his astonishingly various art. Chekhov's stories are, in this sense, his life, tunes that his Russia has put into his head, and are magically sustained.

CHEKHOV

Chapter One

Anton Chekhov was born on January 17, 1860, in the small seaport of Taganrog, a town just outside what are now the boundaries of the Ukraine, on the Sea of Azov in the south of Russia. In the following year Emperor Alexander II had decreed the abolition of serfdom, and it was a matter of pride in the Chekhov family that their peasant grandfather, who had been the manager of the sugar-beet mill and eventually the steward of a large estate in the province of Voronezh, had saved enough money to buy the freedom of his family twenty years before. He had shrewdly educated his sons and put them into trade. Pavel, Chekhov's father, became a bookkeeper in a merchant's office in the larger port of Rostov-on-Don. There, by hard work, he was able at last to marry and to open a general store in Taganrog. His young wife was the daughter of a merchant in the textile trade. Anton was their third son. A daughter and two more sons followed.

With the great difference that Russia was scarcely yet an industrial country and indeed had hardly moved out of its medieval condition, Pavel had much in common with the classic self-made Victorian puritan. He was a fierce believer in Self-Help and the work ethic, a despot in the family, shouting his wife down, ruling his sons by beating them, saying—when his wife protested—that the same had been done to him and that it had made a man of him. Pavel, the slave turned master, was a tall, almost handsome figure with a grizzled beard and a glare in his eyes, a man not to be argued with. All heads were lowered at mealtimes as he hectored the family on their duties. On the wall of the living room was a timetable of the children's tasks, hour by hour, during the day. There were to be no idle minutes, there was to be no playing in the streets. At an early age the children had their duties in the shop. It was open from five in the morning until midnight.

Like the majority of the houses in the poorer parts of the town, the Chekhovs' house had a single story and a tin roof; the store was attached to the house. There was no sanitation: the family had to go to common bogs in a field at the back. For washing there was the communal bathhouse in the town. Where did the family sleep? Behind screens in the living room. Chekhov often slept in a shed where his father kept his lifetime store of newspapers. When the boys started school they had to sit at the counter of the shop, doing their homework, and keeping an eye on the wretched, ill-paid apprentices, who had been trained in the art of short weight and were inclined to steal. In later life when Chekhov was famous he paid for the education of the daughter of one of these lads.

The store sold everything—tallow candles, kerosene lamps, general provisions, tools and sandals. It stank of cheese, herrings and, of course, vodka—sold in a separate room. In the summer the flies swarmed on the greasy counters; rats ran about, and there is a tale that one day a rat drowned in a tub of oil and Pavel, with cunning piety, got a priest in to reconsecrate the oil. Later in his life Anton told the writer Ivan Bunin, whose origins were comparatively genteel, that what he remembered chiefly was the cold nights when he worked in the store, but, with shy pride in his hard times, added: "I sold tallow candles and took the greatest pleasure in wrapping up the icy candles in a scrap of paper."

Pavel's tyranny extended, of course, to the religious life of his family, and here, if not quite a sign of grace, a more affecting aspect of his character appears. The enemy of idleness, he would settle to the common peasant hobby or craft of painting ikons, and this was to have an influence on Nikolay, his second son, who became a talented painter, and on his daughter, Mariya, who when she grew up became a teacher at a Moscow school. More important was Pavel's fanatical addiction to choir singing. He acted as choirmaster in the local church, and he would march his children to choir practice and rehearse them for hours, often until two in the morning. Chekhov was to write of this ordeal with indignation. The Chekhov children appeared like a band of frightened little saints before the congregation. What he detested in this was what he called "the monstrous lie" of this show of enforced saintliness on their part and their father's. To these displays he attributed the early and lasting loss of his religious faith. Yet the artist in Chekhov retained for life his feeling for the rituals of the Orthodox Church and above all for the singing of the ingenious canticles. A few of his finest stories, like *Easter Eve*, *The Artist* and above all the superb *The Bishop*, reflect the profound influence of religious music on his own work. If his prose is plain and neutral, it is nevertheless musical in its architecture and its curious response to sounds.

As a self-appointed choirmaster, Pavel was not disinterested. It was a step to public importance in Taganrog. He rose to the official rank of "merchant of the second Guild," which dated from Peter the Great's creation of an official Russian class system in the grand reforms of the eighteenth century. Through his rank Pavel could claim an important honorary connection with the police. He became a proud figure in official processions, wearing a top hat with the other ruling dignitaries, who lived very much in one another's pockets. If the seaport lived by trade, its habits were oiled by bribery. As a rising tradesman with an eye for financial advantage he saw the importance of education for his children. Here his shrewdness at first misled him.

We must look more closely at Taganrog, as Chekhov evoked it again and again in his stories and letters. With the Crimea on its western shore, the Sea of Azov is linked by a channel to the Black Sea, which gave traders a valuable contact with Turkey and the Mediterranean. The wealth of the port was in the hands of international companies run by Greeks, Italians, Turks, French and British. These foreigners lived grandly apart, in fine streets and in fine houses, whereas the majority of the Russian population were the stevedores and dockworkers who lived in low-built shacks like Pavel's, where the streets were no more than muddy or grass-grown lanes. The Russian houses stank—as Chekhov wrote—of boiled cabbage, of sturgeon baked in sunflower oil and of vodka. One of the popular sports of the rough youths of the town was to catch dogs, give them vodka, tie cans to their tails and chase the maddened animals through the streets.

The foreigners brought some Western graces to the little seaport. The Italians had built a theater and well-known foreign actors and singers appeared there. There was a small park with a bandstand. After the reforms under Alexander II the town had a grammar school. The Greeks too had a school. With an eye to getting his sons into the grain trade, Pavel decided that the Greek school was the place for them. What was the use of the Russian school with its useless classical education? His wife opposed him. She knew little about education, but she did know that boys who graduated at the grammar school might, if they were clever enough, get a grant from the town council which would get them to the university and free them from the nightmare of military service. They might enter the safety of the Civil Service or attain the respectability of doctors or, above all, money-making lawyers. Pavel never listened to his fretful wife. But he had overlooked the obstacle of the Greek language, in which instruction took place. The boys, who were as diligent as their father, were stumped by its difficulties and the quick Greek lads jeered at them. They learned nothing, their marks were poor, and Pavel was appalled. It must be said that for all his money-grubbing he understood the importance of education. Indeed his children were all very able and agreed in later life that they owed their talents to their tedious and stormy father, and their power to feel to their mother. Pavel gave up his dreams of a fortune in foreign trade and moved the boys to the Russian grammar school, and one by one they all went eventually to the university. When Anton's turn came, Pavel had doubts. As an insurance against failure he saw to it that the boy also took lessons in tailoring at the common trade school, and in fact Anton did succeed in making a pair of trousers, fashionably narrow in the leg, for his second brother. That at any rate saved money.

There is a family photograph in which we see the small Anton—he would grow to be as tall as his brothers and father—standing in the neat school uniform, with pride in his stare. He is following his brothers in their journey through classic Greek, Latin, Church Slavonic, Russian, German, religion, geography, mathematics and history. Alexander, the oldest, was heading for mathematics at Moscow University. Nikolay was to follow him, into art. Anton showed no particular bent beyond a gift for hitting off the mannerisms of the masters. One of them may have helped to inspire the schoolmaster in Chekhov's story *The Man in a Case*, a man so afraid of the freedom of private impulse that he puts a stop to everything "unusual" or outside of official control. He represents something that had been a chronic evil in Russian life. Alexander II had introduced reforms in Russia. He had reformed the judiciary, he had created rural district councils—the zemstva—and town councils, he had liberated the serfs, but already there was a feeling that liberal reforms had gone too far. Reaction had begun, and one or two of the masters had the reputation of being government spies on the watch for "dangerous ideas" in the boys. Belikov, in *The Man in a Case*, is a farcical portrait of the type.

One of the natural results of Pavel's sermonizing and his often violent strictness with his wife and his children was to unite them with one another and with their gentle mother. As a girl she had led a wandering life with her father, the traveler in textiles, in many parts of Russia. Her simple mind was full of folklore. She liked to tell the tale of the Crimean War and of how, when Alexander was born in 1855, she had to escape from Taganrog when the Anglo-French fleet bombarded the town. It is commonly the role of the middle child of a large family to be the listener, the watcher, the peacemaker and humorist. Anton loved dressing up, disguises and practical jokes. He was silent at school, but he let himself go with his brothers and sister at home and led the way in making fun of the townspeople of Taganrog. There is a story that he dressed up as a beggar and got money out of his uncle; and another lark—which Pavel would have forbidden if he had seen it—when the boy pretended to be a comic priest being examined by his bishop. Boys were not allowed to go to the town theater without a permit from the school, or without their parents; when he was thirteen, Anton joined a group who dressed up in their fathers' jackets, wore dark glasses, got into the gallery and saw *Hamlet* and Gogol's *The Government Inspector*. He even acted in Gogol's play to entertain the family. Soon he, with his brothers and sister, was sneaking off to private theatricals in the town, and Anton, the born mimic and connoisseur of slapstick, took the lead. And then there was the relief of trips to the country and the sea, and especially to that genial Uncle Mitrofan, when the grocer's shop was forgotten. And, in fact, Chekhov's dark memories of his childhood are less concerned with himself than with the bad effects their severe upbringing had upon his older brothers. They had taken the brunt of their father's temper and been lastingly broken in will by it. Anton took pride in his ability to stare his father in the face when he was likely to be beaten. His will was not broken. The chin is raised in defiance when he stands in his school uniform in the family photographs.

A story called *Difficult People*, written many years later when Chekhov was twenty-six, evokes the family scene in his childhood. One of the boys is leaving home the next day to go on the seven-hundred-mile journey to Moscow University and is asking for money to pay for his fare and keep. The family is at table. The father boils up in a rage of self-pity.

"Take everything!" he shouted in an unnatural voice; "plunder me! Take it all! Strangle me!" He jumped up from the table, clutched at his head and ran staggering about the room. "Strip me to the last thread. Squeeze out the last drop! Rob me! Wring my neck!"

We notice the word "unnatural," which conveys Chekhov's ear for the false in his people.

The boy defies the father. We see him leave the house in the autumn drizzle, his defiance changing to fear, from fear to self-pity and eventually to despair. And then, as so often in Chekhov's stories, an irrelevant sight gives a turning point to the boy's feelings. A rich old lady, a landowner, drives by in an elegant carriage and he bows, smiling.

And at once he caught himself . . . in that smile. . . . Where did it come from if his whole heart was full of vexation and misery? And he thought nature itself had given man this capacity for lying, that even in difficult moments of spiritual strain he might be able to hide the secrets of his nest as the fox and the wild duck do.

For the boy knows the gossip that even in the life of that rich old lady there had been terrible troubles. *Her* father had been exiled by the Tsar, her husband, a gambler, had been ruined, her four sons had turned to the bad. What terrible family scenes there had been! And yet she *smiled*!

The student thought of his comrades, who did not like talking about their families; he thought of his mother, who almost always lied when she had to speak of her husband and children.

The boy turns back to his house and decides to have it out with his father. And so the row starts up again: the timid mother listens speechlessly. The boy shouts:

"Not a dinner or tea passes without your making an uproar. Your bread sticks in our throat. . . . You have worn my mother out and made a slave of her, my sister is hopelessly crushed, while I . . ."

The father shouts back. The boy goes to bed and cannot sleep. Twice his mother comes from behind the screen and makes the sign of the cross over him. He can hear his father pacing the floor all night. At five in the morning the boy gets up once more, calls out good-bye to them all: he is going. As he passes his father's room the father calls out quietly, "The money is on the round table," without turning, as he too says good-bye.

A cold, hateful rain was falling as the labourer drove him to the station. The sunflowers were drooping their heads still lower, and the grass seemed darker than ever.

Chekhov's own drama, when he was sixteen, was more desperate. It was not he who left home in panic and temper. This time the father, indeed the whole family, left suddenly to escape from Taganrog, leaving him behind.

If Pavel was a narrow man, laying down the moral law, he had a Micawber in his nature. The top-hatted figure on the town council and in the processions of Taganrog had had to buy a larger house as the family grew, but he had chosen a bad moment. The railway age had come to Russia late. The larger and more important trading city of Rostov-on-Don at the estuary of the great navigable river Don had become an important railway terminal. There had been a proposal for a branch line to Taganrog but the citizens there had havered about paying the large and necessary bribe for this valuable connection. In the end the town fathers settled for an absurd compromise: a branch line fourteen miles inland from their town. They reckoned that to build a road to the station would be cheaper. In fact building a road cost more. Big ships were turning away from Taganrog, the harbor was neglected and silted up and commerce declined, and the trade of common shopkeepers like Pavel was hit. Soon the aging Pavel went bankrupt. He had borrowed money on note of hand, the lender foreclosed and Pavel could not pay. He was ruined and liable to the law. He fled the town. There was a rumor that he fled secretly to relations in Moscow, hidden in a goods wagon, leaving his wife and children to follow with what family possessions they could carry. The creditor was "merciful" to some extent: he took over house and shop and let the family go, on condition that they left Anton behind as a hostage. Anton was still at school, and the man shrewdly arranged for him to stay on for three years until he graduated, provided that he tutored his son at a cheap rate.

Chapter Two

Anton's situation as a cynically abandoned child is in some respects similar to the fate of Dickens when he was put to work in the blacking factory. There was the difference that Anton was still at school and free of his father's rule and his dread of being beaten. He hated the separation from his brothers and his sister and feared for them: above all he felt responsibility for his helpless mother. This seems to be the moment when he first felt that he was the one with the duty and the wit to replace the father as the practical savior of the family and was no longer the neutral watcher of it. If the strict father had indeed broken the will of his two elder brothers, Anton had conserved his. The lonely but self-reliant boy takes responsibility for the dishes, the pots and pans and the sewing machine his mother has left behind and sends them piecemeal to Moscow when he can afford to do so. Soon, pitiably, and in not very literate letters, his mother is begging him to send money. In addition to tutoring the son of the new shopkeeper, he takes on tutoring other boys at school. He sends the money secretly through a rich Moscow cousin, to whom he writes:

> If I send letters to my mother, care of you, give them to her when you are alone with her, there are things in life which one can confide in one person only, whom one trusts.

And again:

> Please go on comforting my mother, who is both physically and morally broken.

And to his young brother Mikhail he writes a charmingly priggish letter:

> I got your letter when I was fearfully bored and was sitting at the gate yawning, so you can judge how welcome that immense letter was. Your writing is good, and in the whole letter I have not found one mistake in spelling. But one thing I don't like.

He lectures Mikhail for calling himself "your worthless and insignificant brother."

> You recognize your insignificance? . . . Recognize it before God; perhaps, too, in the presence of beauty, intelligence, nature, but not before men.

And then he gives him a precious literary lecture. Harriet Beecher Stowe had been widely read in Russia at the time of the campaign for the liberation of the serfs. Mikhail had said that the story had "wrung tears from my eyes." Anton replies:

I read her once, and six months ago read her again with the object of studying her—and . . . I had an unpleasant sensation which mortals feel after eating too many raisins or currants.

He tells his brother to read *Don Quixote* "by Cervantes, who is said to be almost on a level with Shakespeare," and advises Mikhail to tell his elder brothers to read Turgenev's essay "Hamlet and Don Quixote." "You won't understand it, my dear." He also recommends—and this is a sign of Anton's restlessness and longing for the adventures of travel—Goncharov's *The Frigate Pallada*. The children of the fierce Pavel had all turned out to be readers.

If there is a puritan in Anton, he is enjoying his freedom. He likes his pupil, the creditor's son—a "wild young Cossack of the southern steppe." The boy had an uncle who managed a rich estate, and the two went off and stayed with a primitive family whose incurably talkative father had refused to send the sons to school. They ran wild, shooting every bird in sight, including their own chickens and turkeys and even a pig when the family needed one. Anton called it "wholesale murder" and, years later, he wrote about the family in his famous comic story *The Pecheneg*. The scene was to appear rather differently in *The Steppe*. There were other trips to the steppe. On one he heard for the first time that strange sound of a bucket falling down a mine shaft which haunts other stories and which he was to use again with effect in *The Cherry Orchard*. On another summer trip there was an alarming experience. He loved swimming, and one day he had to be pulled out of the water in agony. He was rushed to a country tavern kept by a Jewish family, who looked after him for the night and then sent him to the grammar school doctor in Taganrog, Dr. Strempf, who diagnosed peritonitis. The recovery was slow, and later in his life Chekhov thought this illness was the cause of the piles and intestinal troubles from which he was to suffer all his life.

The illness was one of those events that become decisive in a youth's life. The doctor told Anton about his profession, and of how he had been trained abroad at Dorpat and in Switzerland. To get abroad! To be trained in Dorpat, even Zurich, as a doctor! The dream grew in his head. Better-off boys at the grammar school became doctors, and his mother wanted her sons to rise above the risks of a tradesman's life.

Anton longed to see his family in Moscow, and at last his eldest brother, Alexander, who was at the university, sent him the fare for the slow seven-hundred-mile journey. When he got there the conditions under which the family lived shocked him. They were packed into a single basement room, where the only sight of the outside world was of the feet of people passing over the grating above the window. The neighborhood was poor and close to the brothel quarter. Pavel had been given a modest job in a warehouse on the other side of Moscow and came home only at weekends. Anton's two older brothers had had to find rooms of their own. In the basement the broken mother earned a few rubles by sewing. It was her conviction that Anton was their only hope. Alexander soon convinced his brother that to think of training to be a doctor in Dorpat or Zurich was out of the question: he would have to be content with Moscow. And indeed, when he had seen the glorious sights of the city and its crowds, Anton was convinced.

He returned to Taganrog. In the two years that followed he worked hard and read enormously. He graduated well enough to get a grant from the town towards his fees at the medical school of Moscow University. He was nineteen.

The photographs of Anton at this time show him to be a tall, energetic young man with the broad face of the Russian peasant. His brown hair is thick and wavy. The fine long eyes have a steady thinking gaze. He is eager for responsibility and to get his family out of that Moscow slum and into decent quarters, especially for the sake of his mother. Money? He will bring with him two rich students who have graduated with him and are going to the university. He will rent rooms to them. His own family must be rescued from debt, from dependence on his father's relations, from the habit of running up bills at the grocer's and butcher's: they must pay cash. There is also the question of educating his sister and his young brothers. He has inherited his father's one virtue: the passion for education. All the Chekhovs are gifted: even his eldest brother, Alexander, who has taken to drink, is an excellent linguist, and Nikolay, who has also drifted into drink and Bohemian life, is a clever painter and is doing caricatures for the Moscow papers. They know Moscow better than he does. In short, Anton has appointed himself head of the family although he has five years at the medical school ahead of him. Although he is sure of himself and soon moves the family into a larger flat, he sees that his grant will vanish into the family pool. He will have to find a spare-time job, and here Alexander is useful. He was trying to write sketches for the comic papers, not with much success, for Alexander is as long-winded as his father. Anton, who, after all, has been the comic entertainer and actor of the family, decides to try his hand. He had started a facetious paper called *The Stammerer* at school.

The assassination of Alexander II in 1881 had been followed by a reaction against his reforms under his successor Alexander III. The censorship was stiffened, and the resourceful Muscovites fell back on their traditional taste for joking, lying and the vulgar. Crude comic magazines were popular. The most popular were *The Alarm Clock* and *The Dragon Fly*, both published in St. Petersburg. You had to be topical and seasonal. You compiled comic calendars, absurd letters of advice; you made sly fun of clerks and officials and newlyweds. Anton makes a drunken bridegroom slash the quilt of the marriage bed so that a cloud of flock pours down on the heads of the crowd outside. There is the tale of people going home to find a coffin in their rooms—an undertaker who is in debt is trying to convince his creditors that there is a boom in his sales; a clerk sneezes over the head of a general in the theater and he pesters the general with apologies—the general has not noticed the sneeze. There are ludicrous scenes in the courts. The thing was to capture the absurd in everyday life, and absurd names were essential. Here Anton was a master. There is a Dyadechkin, a Blinchikov, a Fintifleyev, a top civil servant called Veleleptov whose clerks are Vesisiev and Chernosvinsky. And later on we shall find him inventing the constable Prishibeyev, a pompous policeman so obsessed with unlawful assembly that he will arrest two or three men arguing about the ownership of a dog who has bitten someone in the street; the constable cannot believe it when the judge dismisses the case. Chekhov turned out these things fast and with glee in the middle of his medical studies. Doctors and patients were also victims, of course. The work was very badly paid and some of the magazines evaded payment. If the censor refused to pass a piece, one altered the title and submitted it to another censor known to be idle. The pieces appeared under a pseudonym, Antosha Chekhonte, a comic name given to him by a schoolmaster in Taganrog.

Chekhov was ashamed of this stuff: "The word 'newspaper-writer' means, at very least, a scoundrel. I'm one of them; I work with them; I shake hands with them; I'm even told that I've begun to look like one. . . ." And indeed the shabby young man in the broad-brimmed hat did. "But," he added, "I shan't die as one."

Some of his better things were eventually noticed by Nikolay Leykin, the owner of another Petersburg magazine. Though a secretive, difficult and jealous man, as Chekhov eventually thought, Leykin offered a higher rate than the Moscow journals—eight rubles a line. He wanted Chekhov to write "little stories" and a gossip column on theatrical and social life. The pay was good, but Leykin wanted a monopoly of his work. Chekhov was grateful but he refused to be tied to the new editor, and indeed all his life Chekhov refused to bind himself. For the moment he was grateful for Leykin's interest and concern for the conditions under which he was forced to work. He wrote to Leykin:

I write under the most atrocious conditions. My non-literary work lies before me flaying my conscience un-mercifully. The offspring of a visiting kinsman is screaming in the next room, in another Father is reading aloud [Leskov's] *The Sealed Angel* to mother. . . . Some-one has just wound up the musical box and it's playing "La Belle Hélène." . . . Can you conceive of more atrocious surroundings for a literary man? My bed's taken up by the visiting relation, who keeps coming over to me and engaging me in medical conversation. "My daughter must have colic, that's why she's scream-ing." . . . And when they've had enough of talking medicine, they start on literature.

Many years later Leykin claimed to be the discoverer of Chekhov's talents, and indeed many of the promising "little stories" were written for him. But, like all talented writers, Chekhov was a reading man. He was an admiring if critical reader of Tolstoy and Turgenev: Tolstoy for his almost ani-mal eye for the telling detail and for the portrait of Anna Karenina, Turgenev for his prose style. Dostoyevsky he de-spised for his "shrillness" and his prolonged irrational storms, but there are instances of Dostoyevsky's influence. The more immediate influence at this time was the popular satirical realism of Saltykov-Shchedrin and his one master-piece, the richest and "gloomiest" of Russian novels, *The Golovlyov Family*, with its classic portrait of the traditional Russian hypocrite, Iudushka. Goncharov's famous *Oblomov*, the portrait of the idle Russian landowner, seemed to Chekhov a perverse hymn to idleness, the Russian curse. In his popular older contemporary Leskov, the author of the famous *Lady Macbeth of Mtsensk District*, Chekhov was to have his nearest rival as a copious writer of short stories, but Leskov was religious, indeed he called himself a mystic. Chekhov was an atheist to whom the images and ceremonies of the Orthodox Church were interesting as deeply rooted manifestations of traditional art rather than of acceptable faith.

The young Chekhov was also drawn to the translations of popular French and other European novelists who were fashionable in Russia. He read them in order to parody them. There was a Romantic Hungarian novelist, Mór Jókai, who had written an extravagant novel about the erotic adventures of the daughter of a gypsy violinist in high society in Paris; there were parodies of Victor Hugo and Jules Verne and the famous French writer of detective fiction, Émile Gaboriau, whose ingenuity appealed to Chekhov, as we can see in *The Swedish Match*. In this story he makes rough fun of the mistakes of the inductive method of detection (it turns out that a murder has not occurred: the victim is found to be grossly asleep).

This story was followed by *The Shooting Party*, a combination of melodrama and full-length detective novel, which was run as a newspaper serial in 1884—the anxious year of Chekhov's graduation as a doctor. It was translated into English by A. E. Chamot in 1926 and has recently been reissued with an admiring introduction by Julian Symons, himself a distinguished writer of detective stories. Chekhov took great pains to baffle the reader. The characters are wickedly sensational old-style villainous landowners. The tone is high-flown and lush in its eroticism, a parody of Gaboriau's famous *Monsieur Lecoq* and of the Dostoyevsky of *Crime and Punishment*—Chekhov disliked his "spiritual" melodrama. If the style is one of romantic excess, it must be said that the particularity of landscape and lake and forest has all of Chekhov's feeling for nature. There are glints of the Chekhov to come.

Chapter Three

During the three or four years when he was working for Leykin, Chekhov moved his family eventually into a better house in a more congenial Moscow district: a little red house with a spiral staircase, with carpets on the floor—he had an extravagant taste for carpets—a room for his growing library of books and, at last, a study where he could work alone. We begin to notice several stories of serious merit. If they are comic, they are not crude: they have a core of serious moral insight. This is true of *A Daughter of Albion*, in which a gross landowner is out fishing with the English governess. She cannot speak Russian, he cannot speak English, and he thinks her cold, proud, prim—in short, very English. His line is caught on a root and, hoping to shock her, he takes off his clothes and goes naked into the river to detach it. She is quite indifferent, and when he comes out she simply baits his line for him while he talks to a neighbor. What, in his earlier work, would have been a raw joke now has an unspoken judgment on the landowner's ignorance and coarseness. Slight as the incident is, it "tells."

More pointed is *Anyuta*, in which a medical student and

a painter share a poor sewing girl as a model. We see her in the medic's dirty room. She has taken her blouse off and he is marking her ribs with a piece of chalk as he recites his lesson in anatomy: "The right lung consists of three parts. . . . Upper part on anterior wall of thorax reaches the fourth or fifth rib." The painter comes in to borrow the girl to model for a picture of Psyche and lectures his friend on the filth of his room and tells him that he is not living as "an educated man" and that he ought to make the girl clean up the place. The story now becomes serious. While she is away and he is on his own the medical student takes the painter's words to heart, reflects that one day he will be a successful doctor, even a professor, and that he must get rid of the girl. But how to say this? After an hour she comes back and he blurts out in a muddled way that she knows one day they will have to part and that they'd better do it now. They have been drinking tea; she puts on her coat and with tears in her eyes says, "That's your sugar." This breaks him. He begs her to stay and he starts his comic anatomy lesson again— "The right lung consists of three parts. . . ."

A neat ending to a sentimental story that might have come out of Henri Murger's *Scènes de la Vie de Bohème*? Chekhov had read Murger, as well as Daudet and Maupassant. But look once more at the middle of the story, to the talk of "living like an educated man" and to the crucial moment when she goes off to sit for the painter—the point at which the story has to "turn." The girl comes to life and snaps at "the things I have to put up with here." Chekhov sees that a neat ending will not do. As he often said, the proper ending of a story is always the difficulty. It is solved here, as so often it is in his better work, by "returning" his fiction to real life. As she leaves we hear some unknown man shouting up the stairs of the rooming house: "Grigory! The samovar!"—the indifferent voice of everyday life outside the tale.

Does this story derive from an incident in Chekhov's life as a medical student? It is impossible to say. He had often censured his two older brothers about their behavior to women. It does not match the only account of an early stormy love affair he is known to have had at this time. We know that his mother was eager for him to marry the daughter of the rich haberdasher Gavrilov, who employed Pavel, and that Chekhov rejected the notion with disgust. But a letter from Chekhov to a fellow journalist suggests there were other rumors about a friend of his sister's:

> Now about a fiancée and Hymen. . . . When I speak about a woman I like, I usually prolong the talk to *nec plus ultra*, to the Pillars of Hercules, a trait that has been mine since before my school days. . . . My she is a Jewess. Should a wealthy Jewess have enough courage to embrace Orthodox Christianity with its consequences—very well; if not, it's not necessary. Besides we have already quarreled. . . . Vexed that religion is in her way, she breaks pencils on my desk and photographs—and this is characteristic. A terrible shrew. But . . . finis.

The fiancée, it is thought, was Dunya Efros, a friend of his sister's. Very little is known for certain about the love affairs in Chekhov's life and he himself said there had been very few.

More dangerous was his double life as struggling doctor and comic writer. Moscow was telling on his health. There was an exhausting winter when he covered the lengthy and sensational trial of a corrupt banker. In April 1886 he writes to Leykin, who has complained that he is late with his "copy" and getting lazy: "I am ill. Spitting of blood and weakness . . ."

The next year the family was alarmed. There was tuberculosis on his mother's side of the family. He was to deny for years that he was tubercular, but it is a matter of common observation that consumptives, whether they are evading the knowledge of their disease or not, tend to conceal their fears by doubling the fervor of their imagination and especially their feverish yet detached appetite for living, seeing, feeling and (most noticeable in Chekhov) their denial of what is burning them.

Even though Chekhov pretended, or perhaps thought, that he had merely burst a blood vessel or had trouble with his spleen, it was clear that he needed to get away from his racketing life in Moscow and that he needed a long holiday in the country. Fortunately his brother Ivan had been appointed headmaster of a small school in Voskresensk, about thirty miles from the city. There he was acquainted with the Kiselev family, who had a large estate in the village of Babkino, now Istra. There was a hospital where Anton could work. The Kiselevs were a rich, hospitable and cultivated couple. The husband was the nephew of an ambassador, the wife was the daughter of the director of the Imperial Theater in Moscow. They loved the company of musicians, artists and writers. Mariya Kiseleva herself was a talented writer of children's stories. There was a vacant "cottage" with large rooms which they willingly furnished and rented to the Chekhov family to stay through the spring and summer. For the first time in his life Anton was living on a land-owner's estate. The gardens of the big house were designed in "the English style." There were hothouses. The grounds ran down to a fine river, noted for its excellent fishing, and one looked across to a splendid forest. In the cottage Chekhov had a room to himself where he could write from seven in the morning for three hours. Hearing he was a doctor, the local peasants streamed to his door for treatment. In the afternoons he went fishing with Mariya Kiseleva; in the evenings there were delightful parties at her mansion when they played charades and put on impromptu plays or listened to music. Izaak Levitan, a rising painter, was there, a man who loved practical jokes and disguises. He was recovering from one of his paranoid manias. He and Chekhov liked getting up "comic court trials." One day Anton dressed up as a judge and tried Levitan for "evading military service, keeping an illegal distillery and running a pawnshop." Chekhov listened to the bickerings of the Kiselev children at the card table and was soon making up stories about them and also about an unfortunate dog called Kashtanka, a memory of one of the wretched dogs who had run wild in Taganrog. These stories were despised by the critics, but one notices the excellent recording of children's natures and talk and an imaginative power close to Kipling's in Chekhov's love of animals and birds. As a boy he had passed many hours in the bird market at Taganrog. The mystery of the seasonal migrations of birds excited his wonder all his life. Unlike Levitan, who was a sportsman, Chekhov always refused to shoot a bird.

In the next three years the Chekhov family spent their summers in this paradise. Anton became a close friend of the local doctor and indeed was put in charge of a small hospital when the doctor was away.

There is no doubt that Babkino transformed Chekhov's writing and that his love of the sounds and sights of the country enlarged his powers. Babkino was to become the source and scene of *The Cherry Orchard* years later, and we notice too how quickly he became aware that the extravagant Kiselevs were heading for financial disaster. Mariya Kiseleva's father was reckless in his theatrical enterprises.

For Chekhov the first fruits of Babkino were two remarkable stories, which were noticed at once in Petersburg. Both recall the manner of Turgenev's *Sportsman's Sketches*, his simple yet poetic observation of country life. The first is *The Burbot* (*The Fish* in Constance Garnett's translation), a plain country comedy. Peasants working in the fields on a hot day drop tools and slink off to the river to catch a large fish which is hiding under water among the roots of a tree. One of the men is a hunchback and some are naked and up to their necks in water while the rest shout advice: "Pull him out by the gills, pull him out! . . . Poke him with your finger—you pig's face! . . . Pull it by the lip." The passion and confusion of country sport has seized the peasants. One fellow is nipped by the fish. The others are slapping gnats off their necks. The confusion increases. All work is forgotten. They have deserted the cattle, who run into the river to drink and make things worse. Presently the master of the estate comes down to find out what is going on. The beauty of it is that the master is dressed in his Persian dressing gown, carrying a newspaper (one of Chekhov's incidental touches that tell us much about the landowner's idle life). He calls up the coachman to help, but that fails. So, with dignity, the master gets his clothes off and jumps naked into the pool to show the yokels he knows the trick. Skillfully he pulls the fish out at once. It is an enormous fish, a ten-pounder. He displays it on the flat of his hand. Then, suddenly, the fish jumps into the air and dives back into the stream for good. That is all, but the tale of the master's comeuppance will be told and improved upon for years. It will become a local legend: Chekhov has caught the confusion on a memorable hot day forever.

The other story of the new Chekhov is *The Huntsman*. This is more subtle in its psychological and social observation. Yegor is a handsome peasant loner, a privileged gamekeeper, vain of his looks and his instinctive shooting skills. He has been raised to the status of the indispensable steward at the big house: boasts that he eats "landowner's food." We see him "ambling along the road" by the woods. Presently the young peasant wife whom he has deserted and rarely troubles to visit timidly calls out to him. She sees he has shot a grouse. She knows he will not come to the village to see her. Why? Is it true that he has taken up with another girl? He has always despised women and their ties. He is a "wild man."

"You could have called in just once," she says.

"What for?" he asks. His freedom cannot be "taken." She says she has "worn her eyes out" waiting for him. She has not seen him for a year and even then he had been drunk and had beaten her.

"Waiting—what for?" he says.

She replies, "Not to do anything, of course, but it is your household, after all. . . . Just to see how everything is. . . . You are the head."

She sits down at a distance, talking to him. They have been married for twelve years. "In church," she says. "Not freely," he says. He tells her she's no more than a peasant working in the fields, living in dirt, that she wears bast shoes and her back is bent. And he stands by his superiority, his fame as a huntsman. He's in the money. He is no longer a peasant. He's free. If they were to take his gun away he'd easily take to horse dealing. "Once that free spirit's got into a man there's no winkling it out," he says. He does not admit or deny that he has built a hut for another girl. He gives his wife a ruble and goes off. The end of the story? No. What is the last sight of a loved man like? Once more Chekhov is the collector of moments "that tell," as if continuing human life is made of them:

Pale and still, she stands there like a statue, and her eyes devour every stride he takes. But now the red of his shirt merges with the dark of his trousers, his strides become invisible, his dog cannot be distinguished from his boots. Only his little cap can be seen then. . . . Suddenly Yegor turns off sharply . . . into the scrub and his cap disappears among the green. "Goodbye,

Yegor Vlasych!" whispers Pelageya and rises on tiptoe to try and catch a last glimpse of his little white cap.

This year was dramatic for Chekhov. *The Huntsman* appeared in Petersburg in 1885, not in Leykin's humorous journal but in a superior publication, *The Petersburg Gazette*. Chekhov, who had been despised by serious critics, was acclaimed. He was at the point when a young writer becomes more than "promising" to elders. He received a long letter from Dmitry Grigorovich, an established novelist of the older generation, who noted Chekhov's innate sense of form and his "feeling for the plastic." He said Chekhov had "real talent . . . a talent which sets you far above other writers of the younger generation." Chekhov would be guilty of "a grievous moral sin" if he did not live up to these hopes. This was in March 1886. Chekhov respected but did not admire the work of Grigorovich, but he was grateful. He confesses, too fulsomely perhaps,

> If I have a gift which one ought to respect I confess before the pure candour of your heart that hitherto I have not respected it. . . . In the course of the five years that I have been knocking about from one newspaper office to another . . . I soon got used to looking down upon my work. . . . This is the first reason. The second is that I am a doctor, and am up to my ears in medical work.

He admits his attitude to his work has been foolish and casual.

I don't remember a *single* story over which I have spent more than twenty-four hours. . . . [I am] working against time.

He says nothing about the cheap journalism he was writing at the same time.

Earlier, in the autumn of 1885, Leykin advised Chekhov that the time had come for meeting the crucially important literary society of Petersburg, the capital of Russian literature. Chekhov said that he could not afford even the fare: the family eats up all his money, which is "as short as cats' tears." He had to pay for the running of his Moscow house, he owed rent for the summer cottage at Babkino; the sacred Christmas and Easter festivals always ruined him and, in any case, money always ran through his fingers.

A few months later he gave in, defying the dangerous December climate, and went with Leykin to meet the man who was effectively to change his life: Aleksey Suvorin, the millionaire publisher and owner of *New Time* (*Novoe Vremya*), the most conservative and important newspaper in Russia, the only one that could stand comparison with the great papers of Europe. He had had his eye on Chekhov's better stories; he would pay twice the rate Leykin paid him. Suvorin wanted the exclusive rights to Chekhov's work, but on that Chekhov would not agree. Suvorin gave way.

Chapter Four

Chekhov's friends were, like himself, liberals. They were appalled that he had gone over to a man notorious for his reactionary politics. How could he be so self-seeking as to give himself to the enemy? Chekhov declared that his independence was guaranteed, but for years his earnest friends were skeptical. They were even more astonished when they saw the relationship between the twenty-six-year-old writer and the rich entrepreneur in his fifties become a close friendship, and saw the older man become the attentive pupil of the younger. Both men came from the volatile south. The self-made Suvorin had started life as a humble schoolteacher. He had moved on to buying a dying provincial newspaper at the time of the Russo-Turkish War and had transformed it by getting direct vivid dispatches from the front which exposed the grievances of the officers and men. The paper became popular with the powerful military interests at once. Suvorin had been arrested for publishing unauthorized reports and had been sent to prison for a few months. On his release he took advantage of the railway age, founded *New*

Time and saw that it was distributed at every railway station in Russia. He got the monopoly of the bookstalls and, astonishingly, started the publication of cheap editions of the Russian classics. He was an eager autodidact. He himself had tried to write novels, but seeing more money in the theater, he had turned to it and had a small success with popular plays simply because he could afford to buy the most successful actors and actresses. He had read, and met, Tolstoy, Turgenev, Dostoyevsky and—surprising in a conservative—had taken the trouble to meet and read Chernyshevsky, the revolutionary socialist and author of the notorious *What Is to Be Done?* which was the bible of the radicals. The author had been sent to prison and then exiled for a long term in Siberia.

There is commonly an element of naïveté in the character of self-made men. In the long friendship between Suvorin and Chekhov, Suvorin is the earnest, hospitable man of the world, Chekhov is the bright young teacher. Chekhov stayed with Suvorin in Petersburg and, in time, traveled with him all over Europe and stayed with him and his family in his villa in the Crimea. The friendship, generous on Suvorin's part, did not decline until, in old age, Suvorin in one of his anti-Semitic fits attacked Dreyfus and Zola.

Chekhov is one of the outstanding natural letter writers in Russian literature and his long correspondence with Suvorin is forthright, amusing and, above all, revealing. Suvorin's replies have most unfortunately been lost. It was to Suvorin that Chekhov wrote the often quoted utterance which displays his pride:

What aristocratic writers take from nature gratis the less privileged must pay for with their youth. Try to write a story about a young man—the son of a serf, a former grocer, choirboy, schoolboy and university student, raised on respect for rank, kissing the priests' hands, worshipping the ideas of others and giving thanks for every piece of bread, receiving frequent whippings, making the rounds as a tutor without galoshes, brawling, torturing animals, enjoying dinners at the houses of rich relatives, needlessly hypocritical before God and man merely to acknowledge his own insignificance—write about this young man who squeezes the slave out of himself, drop by drop, and who, one fine morning, finds that the blood coursing through his veins is no longer the blood of a slave but that of a real human being.

Very early Suvorin is concerned because his young genius is splitting his life in two as a doctor and a writer. Chekhov replies:

You advise me not to hunt after two hares and not to think of medical work. I do not know why one should not hunt two hares even in the literal sense. . . . I feel more confident and more satisfied with myself when I reflect that I have two professions. . . . Medicine is my lawful wife and literature my mistress. . . . There is no discipline in me.

Suvorin had a rather solemn interest in intellectual problems. For example, he complains that in *The Horse Thieves*

Chekhov had not taken sides and solved the problem. Chekhov replies:

> You confuse two things: *solving a problem* and *stating a problem correctly*. It is only the second that is obligatory for the artist. In *Anna Karenina* and *Yevgeny Onegin* not a single problem is solved, but they satisfy you completely because all the problems are correctly stated in them.

Suvorin protests that this looks like indifference to good and evil. Isn't horse stealing wrong? Chekhov replies there is no need for him to say horse stealing is wrong: everyone has known that for ages. His job is simply to say what these people are like.

> These people are not beggars, but well-fed people with their own vocation—horse stealing for them isn't just stealing, it's a passion.

To depict a horse stealer in seven hundred lines is partly a matter of technique. A writer must unself himself and "must speak and think in their tone and must feel as a fellow-spirit, otherwise the images will become blurred."

Suvorin certainly freed Chekhov from Leykin and journalism by paying him highly, but this did not immediately break Chekhov of the habit of writing too much. Petersburg readers had a taste for erotic stories, which would not have been publishable in Moscow. In *The Witch* the impotent, superstitious and jealous sexton of a lonely country church has come to believe that his wife has invoked the blizzard that rages round his filthy hut. She has put a lamp in the window in order to lure the mail drivers to her bed. We see in her the brooding of frustrated sexuality. The drivers indeed arrive and the impotent husband gloats on their indifference to her: the men are simply lost and are afraid of being too late for the mail train. Not a Chekhovian joke: Chekhov has created unmistakably the sullenness of desire and the determination of the men to ignore an easy seduction.

In *Agafya* Chekhov seems to be rewriting *The Huntsman*, but here the man is simply a handsome layabout peasant who refuses to work and lies in the woods all day. Village women who are under his sexual spell bring him food. How is sexual feeling evoked? Partly from the conniving innocence of the landscape, the peasants' scanty talk and the gaze of the girl to whom the layabout gives vodka. We know also that she must get away quickly before her husband comes in by the train that will soon be signaled. We watch the signal light change from red to green. She overstays her time. Chekhov makes it clear what has gone on between the layabout and the girl by the remarkable account of her flight across the field to face her husband:

She moved in zigzags, then she moved her feet up and down without going forward, bending her knees and stretching out her hands, then she staggered back. When she had gone another hundred paces she looked around once more and sat down.

The defect of the story is that the narrator is outside it, but at least he sees that flight. The idle peasant does not even look. Finally, defiantly, she jumps up again to face her husband, knowing that he will beat her. There is the story: the willful idleness of love, the physical sight of making up the mind to face the price. If Chekhov is a master of moods they are almost always enacted.

Two stories are exercises in the manner of Maupassant's *The Necklace*—a subject which has exercised many short-story writers, including Henry James. In *An Upheaval* we see a young au pair girl coming into her bedroom and catching her employer's wife rummaging in her drawer; the excuse of the lady is that her jewelry has been stolen. The girl is indignant and decides to leave the house at once. One of Chekhov's grim family luncheons follows. Privately the husband begs the girl to stay and, in the end, even goes down on his knees and confesses that *he* has sold his wife's jewelry. "If you go," he says to the girl, "there won't be a human face left in the house." The containing theme is that this pretentious bourgeois family have created "a life of lies," and the girl leaves.

The Chorus Girl is a variation on the same theme: an hysterical wife knows an actress is her husband's mistress and goes to the girl's flat begging her to hand over the jewelry her husband has given her. The family is ruined. The girl says that all the husband has given her are a few cheap trinkets and, shocked that a *lady* should go down on her knees and beg, she throws the cheap stuff other men have given her at the wife, who goes off in triumph. The husband, hiding in the next room, comes out storming because he is shamed by the sight of his wife begging to such a creature, and he breaks with her. We notice the care with which Chekhov avoids the neat ending. The story must be returned to the inexplicable continuing human experience. The girl is left weeping and crying:

> She remembered how three years ago a merchant had beaten her for no sort of reason, and she wailed more loudly than ever.

Two stories of this period are far more important: *Easter Eve* and *Art*. They take us back, no doubt, to scenes of Chekhov's childhood, but there is a new musical element in his art—"the necessary tune" in the head that prompts the act of writing. In *Easter Eve* the anonymous narrator is on the riverbank waiting for the ferryman to take him across to an Easter celebration. A peasant shouts and is answered, not by a man but by the hoarse slow peal of a bell "as from the thickest string of a double bass." Then the sound of a cannon shot rolls over the fields "behind me" and before the first peal has died away, a second and a third. Presently a humble monk comes across in the ferry. He is sad. Why? "Even in the time of great rejoicing, a man cannot forget his sorrows." His sorrow is that a monk called Nikolay has died, a simple unlettered man with a genius for composing hymns of praise. The heart of the story lies in the account of how traditional canticles must be put together. The monk says:

"Anyone who writes canticles must know the life of the saint to perfection, to the least trivial detail [and] one must make them harmonize with the other canticles and know where to begin and what to write about. . . . The first line must always begin with the 'angel.' . . . what matters is the beauty and sweetness of it. . . . For brevity [the composer] packs many thoughts into one phrase. . . . there must be flowers and lightning and wind and sun . . . and every exclamation ought to be put so as to be smooth and easy for the ear. . . . It is not simply 'heavenly flower,' but 'flowers of heavenly growth.' "

Is the artist, then, a sort of monk? Far from it, as we see in the other Easter story, *Art*. At Easter the villagers have the tradition of building what they call a Jordan, which will stand on the ice in the middle of their frozen river. They are craftsmen. They know how to carve out the clumsy object, which combines a lectern with an enormous cross that can be seen rising above the village roofs. Before he starts work the artist looks on, curses the villagers and goes off to get drunk. His task is to glorify the grotesque object, but he cannot be found until the last minute, when he is very drunk. What has he been doing? He has been preparing his colors. He has been patiently making them out of beet-root leaves and onion skin, and he starts furiously yet carefully to paint. The rudimentary Jordan becomes a shaft of dazzling light and now the unmanageable man gazes with humility at his creation.

A fable, of course, but notice that everything in the village festival is there and that the narrative has been given the necessary fever by being written in the present tense. It is said that Chekhov used his hard-drinking, playacting and paranoid friend, the painter Levitan, for his model in this story.

We have already been struck by the fact that the so-called connoisseur of moods is almost invariably concerned with the métier, the trades and professions of his characters, whether they are peasants, workmen, doctors, lawyers or landowners. What does occupation do to a man's nature? In *The Kiss*, the one long story he wrote in his 1887 summer at Babkino, there is an extraordinary example of Chekhov's power of absorbing the mystique of an occupation yet avoiding tedious documentation. At Babkino a brigade of artillery was stationed. It was not difficult to note the characteristics of officers and men, to catch their work, their duties, their talk in the mess, the difference between their preoccupations on the march, their care for their equipment; their "mystique" is another matter. Chekhov had read Tolstoy and Lermontov and already knows that an army is a migrant culture. He may have been told the incident of the story by a general he had met at the Kiselevs, but it would have lost all perspective if he had not, by a mixture of observation and meiosis, put a regiment on duty plainly before us as human beings.

The story opens lightly with a party. The retired General Von Rabbek, local lord of the manor, has invited the officers to it. They are keen, of course, to meet the ladies. There are drinks and there is dancing. The soldiers throw themselves into the fun—all except Staff Captain Ryabovich. He can't dance or play billiards; he is a short ugly fellow who wears spectacles and has lynxlike whiskers and is shut up in himself. He wanders about with gloomy curiosity over the grand house, walks into a room, which is in darkness. Suddenly he has an experience that will haunt him for years. A girl rushes into the dark room, cries out "At last!," kisses him, then gives a scream and runs away. She has mistaken him for someone else. The ugly, shy little staff captain is transformed. He feels suddenly proud. He struts back to the ballroom and tries to guess, by a perfume or a voice, who the girl was. He fails to find out, and from now on we see a life of fantasy beginning.

The evening comes to an end. The soldiers leave and take a shortcut through the woods to their billets, shouting and laughing. No doubt, says Chekhov, they were wondering whether *they* would someday have a mansion like the general's and whether they would be rich enough to have fine gardens and woods like these. But Ryabovich is lost in his obsession. The stars are out and their reflection trembles, dissolves and forms again in the stream he crosses, just as the misleading kiss reflects in his life. He hears—as so often occurs in Chekhov's landscape—"the plaintive cry of drowsy snipe" and "a nightingale in full song," and one of the vulgar soldiers says, "How about that! . . . the little rascal doesn't give a damn!" Here we notice one of the differences between Turgenev and Chekhov: in Chekhov the sights and sounds of nature are seen and heard by *people*. In Turgenev they are seen and heard by the detached author for their own beautiful sake. When distant lights shine through the trees, for example, Ryabovich thinks the lights know his secret. Back at the billet he is brought instantly down to earth. The batman is reporting to the commander: "Darling's foot was injured at yesterday's re-shoeing, sir. The vet put on clay and vinegar."

The next day the brigade moves off with its guns and Ryabovich is split between his daydreams and his full efficiency as an automatic soldier. As the brigade rumbles down the road the military life "makes sense" to Ryabovich, perhaps the only thing that does make sense! He knows that the rumbling procession of guns has to be led by a vanguard of four men with drawn sabers, that after them come the "singers"—like torchbearers in a funeral procession:

[Ryabovich] has known for ages why a sturdy bombardier rides alongside the officer at the head of each battery and why he is given a special name. . . . [he] knows that the horses on the left, on which the riders are mounted, have one name and those on the right another. . . . Behind the driver come the two wheel-horses. On one of them sits a rider with yesterday's dust on his back and a clumsy, very funny-looking piece of wood on his right leg; Ryabovich knows the purpose of this piece of wood and does not find it funny. Every single rider brandishes his whip mechanically and from time to time gives a shout.

The gun carriage itself is ugly and absurd: it has teapots and soldiers' packs hanging all over it.

Bringing up the rear is the baggage train, and striding thoughtfully beside it, drooping his long-eared head, is a highly sympathetic character: the donkey, Magar, imported from Turkey by one of the battery commanders.

At midday—and how long and monotonous Russian days are; in them daydreams drag on, are interrupted and start again—the brigade general drives down the column in his barouche and shouts something that no one grasps. Ryabovich and others gallop up to him. "Any sick?" asks the general from his barouche and tells Ryabovich his breechings look slack. Such is military servitude.

Eventually the brigade returns from its exercises to its base near the manor house. Locked in his daydreams, Ryabovich cannot resist making a secret trip alone across the river, through the woods, for a closer look at the house. He knows his dream of finding the girl is futile. The whole world, the whole of life, strikes the ugly Ryabovich as an unintelligible joke directed against himself. It seems likely, given his dullness and the routine of military life, that his isolation will be lasting. He will be locked in himself.

As an innovator in the writing of short stories, especially in his mastery of nostalgia and mood, Chekhov knew that his great predecessors were novelists who had addressed themselves to questions like the emergence of Russia from its prolonged medieval condition. The patrician Turgenev had made his stand for the liberation of the serfs and the example of Western civilization. Dostoyevsky had been sent to Siberia for his part in an alleged revolutionary conspiracy but had ended in denouncing the Western socialist idea and its materialism. Tolstoy, after his conversion, had turned to simple Bible teaching and to the doctrine of nonresistance to evil by force. There was now a new radical generation who were growing up as Russia became, to some degree, industrialized. In the older generation one was judged by one's "convictions"; in Chekhov's by one's "tendency." There is a letter to the elderly poet Aleksey Pleshcheyev, who had in his time been sent to prison in Siberia, in which Chekhov describes his stand:

> I am afraid of those who look for a tendency between the lines and insist on seeing me as necessarily a liberal or a conservative. I am not a liberal, not a conservative, not a gradualist, not a monk, not an indifferentist. I should like to be a free artist and nothing more and I regret that God has not given me the power to be one. I hate lying and violence, whatever form they may take. . . . Pharisaism, stupidity and tyranny reign not only in shopkeepers' homes and in lock-ups alone: I see them in science, in literature, in the younger generation. . . . I regard trade-marks and labels as prejudicial. My holy of holies is the human body, health, intelligence, talent, inspiration, love and absolute freedom—freedom from force and falsehood. . . .

Here it is important to look at a story called *On the Road* and a play, *Ivanov*, which derives from it, which were written in one of Chekhov's summers at Babkino. In both, the disastrous history of an educated man's search for "convictions" are dramatically examined. *On the Road* is one of the Chekhov's finest dramatic stories. It is true that it brings to mind an encounter towards the end of Turgenev's *Rudin*—perhaps modeled in part on Bakunin. Like Rudin, Chekhov's hero, Likharyov, is one of those torrential talking egoists, the old-style "superfluous man," but now updated. He is a young ruined landowner who has given up his estate, and we see him traveling with his tiny daughter and stopping at a rough roadside inn. A gentlewoman is sheltering there too. She has been on a round of visits to friends in the province. Instantly he pours out a nonstop confession, the history of his changing "convictions," his sins, his unforgivable behavior to his dead wife. Chekhov notes, "To an educated Russian his past is always beautiful, his present a tale of calamity." Likharyov tells her he has gone from faith in God to faith in the Sciences, chemistry, zoology. He has been, in politics, a Slavophile, a nihilist, to the point of shooting a gendarme. He had once converted a nun to nihilism; he boasts of his success with women. During these changes of mind and fortune his wife had never left his side. "A noble sublime slavery," he says. ". . . the highest meaning of woman's life." Now she is dead. Only once does he pause: his tiny daughter has been put to rest wrapped in a blanket on the floor and the exhausted child calls out, "He won't let me sleep with his talking." He soothes the child and the night passes. In the morning he goes on again. What is he going to do? He has made a decision. He is traveling to Siberia to work in a coal mine.

The lady gets ready to leave. She thinks about secretly slipping money into his pocket but then goes off on her sleigh. She has been dangerously under his spell.

> Not only in her heart but even in her spine she felt that behind her stood an infinitely unhappy man, lost and outcast.

Likharyov watches her settle into her sleigh and drive off.

> She looked back at Likharyov as though she wanted to say something to him. He ran up to her but she said nothing to him, she only looked at him through her long eyelashes with little specks of snow on them.

That is all.

The Kiselevs admired the story. They saw that it would make a remarkable one-act play, but they knew the censor would never allow the sight of a gentlewoman spending the night at a remote inn, however innocently, with a man she did not know. That scene must go. Chekhov saw a full-length play in the traveler's past, and *On the Road* is the source of his first long play, *Ivanov*. Likharyov is now Ivanov. We see him on his estate, married to a Jewish wife, who has been disinherited by her rich parents and who is now dying. His bailiff has been robbing him for years and he is ruined: worse—while waiting for his wife to die he has taken up with an "advanced" young girl, whom he plans to marry. The only objection to the marriage comes from a Dr. Lvov, who is disgusted by Ivanov's cynicism and publicly denounces him. But Ivanov is also trapped by his dishonest bailiff, who is perpetrating a fraud, and his master has been too weak to sack him. The question is: Will Ivanov be base enough, fool enough and weak enough to marry the young girl the moment the unloved wife dies?

The play made an impression in St. Petersburg chiefly because it was played by rhetorical actors of the old school, who stormed through it, treating it as a melodrama, for at the end Ivanov is driven to shoot himself on the morning of his wedding day: they turned Ivanov into a villain and Dr. Lvov into his righteous judge. Suvorin thought they were right, and indeed at first glance we shall more than half agree with him, but in his letters to Suvorin, Chekhov gives a far more interesting and convincing account of his intentions. Ivanov, he says, was not a monster:

His past is beautiful. . . . There is not, or there hardly is, a single Russian gentleman or University man who does not boast of his past. The present is always worse than the past. Why? Because Russian excitability has one specific characteristic: it is quickly followed by exhaustion. . . . [He feels] only an indefinite feeling of guilt. It is a Russian feeling. Whether there is a death or illness in his family, whether he owes money or lends it, a Russian always feels guilty. . . . [Ivanov says:] "My thoughts are in a tangle, my soul is in bondage to a sort of sloth, and I am incapable of understanding myself." . . . To exhaustion, boredom, and the feeling of guilt add one more enemy: loneliness.

The case against Ivanov is made by the young puritanic Dr. Lvov. Is Lvov right? Chekhov replies to Suvorin that the doctor

is the type of an honest, straightforward, hotheaded, but narrow and uncompromising man. . . . Anything like breadth of outlook or spontaneous feeling is foreign to Lvov. He is cliché incarnate, bigotry on two feet . . . he judges everything prejudicially. He worships those who shout, "Make way for honest labor!" Those who don't are scoundrels and exploiters. . . . When he reads [Turgenev's] *Rudin* he just has to ask himself "Is Rudin a scoundrel or not?" . . . Lvov is honest. . . . If need be, he will bomb a carriage, slap a school inspector's face. . . . He never feels conscience pangs—it is his mission as "an honest toiler" to destroy "the powers of darkness."

What about Ivanov's dying wife? She loves him so long as he is excited, because his enthusiasm is brilliant and he is as heated as Lvov is. But when Ivanov grows misty to her she cannot understand him and will soon turn on him. The young girl to whom Ivanov turns is the latest example of the "educated woman." What attracts her is the duty of rescuing Ivanov from his depression and putting him on his feet and making him happy.

The most interesting critical comment on *Ivanov* will be found in Ronald Hingley's book on Chekhov. Hingley turned to a Russian source, Ovsyaniko-Kulikovsky's *History of the Russian Intelligentsia*, which says that, as a doctor,

Chekhov was making a medical study of Ivanov's "neurasthenia"; the play is "a medical tragedy."

There are burly, ignoble and shameless characters in the play, especially the bailiff, Borkin, who has cynically exploited Ivanov's weaknesses. Like other landowners, Ivanov is always in debt. Borkin, who has robbed him, invites him to recoup by swindling. He suggests, for example, that Ivanov should buy the opposite bank of the river, beyond the boundary of his estate. This will give him the right to dam the river and build a mill, which will bankrupt the factories below the dam. The owners will have to bribe him handsomely to prevent the scheme. (Everyone knows what Borkin once bought up herds of cattle during an epidemic, insured them, then infected them and collected the insurance.) When Lvov calls Ivanov a scoundrel, it is either fatal to his tottering brain or stimulates him to a new paroxysm, and in shooting himself, he sentences himself.

Chapter Five

Although Suvorin had freed Chekhov from the need to live as a facile popular hack, Chekhov's emergence was not sudden. Life in Moscow was expensive and the demands of what he called his "abnormal family," of which he had appointed himself the head, were heavy and Moscow was bad for his health. His two younger brothers were settling into decent jobs; his sister was dedicated to her teaching career, but Nikolay had given up painting and become a drunken vagrant. In a famous letter Chekhov became a kind of Dr. Lvov, lectured Nikolay item by item on the behavior one must follow if one was to be regarded as a "cultured man." Alexander, the eldest of the brothers, who had introduced Chekhov to the comic magazines, had given up writing and had drifted into a minor job as a customs official, which he soon lost, and was living in careless squalor with a common-law wife in St. Petersburg. Early in March 1887 Chekhov found an hysterical telegram from Alexander saying there was a typhus epidemic and that he and his wife were dying of it, and begging Anton to save them. Anton himself had had a hemorrhage recently but he traveled third class in the train, coughing over the bad cigarettes he smoked, and arrived to find Alexander perfectly well but hysterical in a filthy flat. Only his wife was ill, and not with typhus. Anton treated her and she recovered. Alexander was in fact even deeper in drink than Nikolay and was chasing another woman. He had the nerve to demand that Anton take his children off his hands and look after them in Moscow.

In any crisis Chekhov's instinct was to get away. He was in any case an instinctive nomad. He went to see Suvorin. He told him that he wanted to go to the south, to the scene of his childhood, and write a novel. Suvorin at once advanced the money. Chekhov was to pass through detestable Taganrog, but he was returning not to the memories of his father's shop, where he had been abandoned as a schoolboy, but to his genial uncle Mitrofan and the nearby country of the Donets steppe, where he would be free and happy. We are alarmed to hear that he had the idea of making this place the background of a topical novel on the theme of the wave of child suicides that was sweeping across Russia. He wrote:

> Russian life bashes the Russian till you have to scrape him off the floor, like a twenty-ton rock. In Western Europe people perish because life is too crowded and close; in Russia they perish because it is too spacious. . . .

That spaciousness he was now seeking in the steppe. It strikes us that he would be making one of those returns to the source of his imagination in childhood which have so often revived the gifts of harassed writers. Chekhov split Suvorin's money, leaving half to his sister for the family, and in April 1887 set off by train.

In letters to his sister he chatters on about his fellow passengers, people interested only in the price of flour, on the way to Serpukhov; they were livelier after Kursk. There was a jokey landowner from Kharkov; a lady who had just had an operation in Petersburg; an officer from the Ukraine, a general in uniform whose arguments on social questions were surprisingly "sound, short and liberal"; a police officer who was an old battered sinner who growled like a dog. At Slavyansk a railway inspector got on and told them how the Sevastopol railway company had stolen three hundred carriages from the Azov line and painted them in its own company's color. (Chekhov used the incident in *Cold Blood*.) Then comes the wild scent of the steppe. He hears the birds singing and sees his "old friends" the ravens flying over the barrows. At one station, "at an upper window sits a young girl in a white blouse, beautiful and languid." Chekhov puts on his pince-nez; she puts on hers; the two gaze at each other. That will be evoked in a remarkable prose poem, *The Beauties*. He is in "devilishly, revoltingly fine form"; there are more Ukrainians, oxen, ravens, white huts, telegraph wires, daughters of landowners, farmers, red dogs; trees flit by as he drinks his vodka and eats rissoles and pies. At eight in the evening he is at last in Taganrog. A shock: all the houses look ruinous and flattened. It's a town "like Herculaneum and Pompeii"—where he had never been—and when he finds his uncle, the family, even the rats in the storehouse, are fast asleep. He has to sleep on a short sofa and his long legs hang down on the floor. At five in the morning he wakes up. The family are still asleep.

The house pretends to luxury but there are no cuspidors and there is no water closet. He hates Taganrog; still, the Grand Street smells of Europe. The upper-class people, all Greek and Polish, walk on one side of the street, the Russian poor on the other. Now he is suffering from diarrhea (caused by his aunt's rich cooking) and inflammation of his leg—"my infirmities are countless." He is drinking more than he should. The young ladies of the town are not bad-looking, but they move abruptly and behave frivolously with him. In general, he says, they fall in love and elope with actors, guffaw and whistle for their dogs. Taganrog is still plagued by dogs. He goes on to Morskaya Stantsiya and he eats caviar for breakfast at seventy kopecks a pound, and marvelous butter. But sleeping? "The devil only knows what I haven't spent the night on: on beds with bugs, on sofas, settees, boxes." Then he is off by train to a Cossack wedding; everyone drinks, including himself. Millions of girls rush about in a crowd like sheep. "One . . . kept striking me . . . with her fan and saying 'Oh you naughty man!' while at the same time her face wore an expression of fear." Chekhov, the Moscow worldling, teaches her to say to her swains, "How naïve you are!"

Another train, and from the siding he sees the boundless steppe and its ancient grave mounds by moonlight. At Ragozina Balka he stays with a large wild Cossack family—the one his pupil took him to stay with in his teens. The tedious father is still running his farm on "scientific" principles, i.e., by a new book he has picked up. This has led to a Cossack war on all wild life.

> They kill sparrows, swallows, . . . magpies, ravens so that they should not eat the bees; they kill the bees so that they should not damage the blossoms of the fruit trees, and fell trees so that they should not impoverish the soil. . . . [At night] my hosts fire rifles at some animal that is damaging the economy.

And once more there is no water closet. You go out to the hills. This is more material for *The Pecheneg*—his story about the greatest rural, demented, speculative bore in Russia.

Chekhov has gone lame. More trains. In agony he reaches the monastery at Svyatyye Gory. Here the dogs bark, the frogs croak, the nightingales sing, there are pilgrims. He meets a converted Jew. Back again to Taganrog, and he writes to a friend who is an architect: "If I were as gifted an architect as you I would raze it." The Taganrog that seriously remained in his mind was "stark" Asia,

> such an Asia that I cannot believe my eyes. The sixty thousand inhabitants busy themselves with eating, drinking, procreating, but no newspapers and no books. . . . the fruits of the earth abound, but everyone is apathetic. Yet they are musical, they have fantasy and wit; they are high-strung and sensitive, but all is wasted.

What about the masterpiece? He goes back to Moscow to write it. The theme of the child suicides is scrapped: will the book simply be a work of travel, an "encyclopaedia of the Steppe"? Some words of Camus come to one's mind: "one of our contemporaries is cured of his torment by contemplating a landscape." Chekhov is recovering his childhood imagination.

The Steppe is the account of a journey seen through the eyes of a very young boy, a memory conjured out of himself. If the long book seems to be no more than a series of interlocking incidents, it is really a sustained prose poem and the longest "story" Chekhov ever wrote. Above all, it evokes the mysterious, fated feeling that Russians felt and still feel about the vast empty distances of central Russia and their outlying parts on the edge of the Ukraine in the south, just as the tableland, or steppe, of Castile, with its isolated flat-topped hills and the wide empty distances, haunts the Spaniards. Spain and Russia: they echo each other. From the Russian steppe something has passed permanently into the Russian mind and Russian literature: the sensation of endless time, mysterious in its primitive beginnings. It was natural for Russian writers of Chekhov's time to think of the steppe as the country of Don Quixote, and Chekhov had been deep in Cervantes from his boyhood. There was also for him the romantic Russian counterpart in Gogol's story of *Taras Bulba*. Literature grows out of literature as well as out of life: the difference between *The Steppe* and Gogol's magnificent book is that Gogol was glorifying Cossack history, whereas Chekhov stuck to a young boy's response to the sights and tales of the road.

So we see the boy, Yegorushka, who is the hero, taken on a long journey from Taganrog to boarding school in far-off Kiev. He is whimpering in misery, in a springless carriage, in the company of his uncle Kuzmichov, a stern wool merchant, and the pious Father Christopher, who tries to teach the boy history and religion. The boy sits on the box and clings to the arm of the coachman, who does not stop whipping up his pair of bay horses. They drive out of Taganrog past the brickfields and the town prison, where, because it is Easter, the boy had been to give Easter eggs to the convicts. A prisoner had given him "a pewter buckle of his own making." A small comfort. The uncle is mostly silent, except when he is arguing with the delightful chattering priest—Chekhov's Sancho Panza—who is on to an illegal deal in wool himself for dubious "family reasons," but really for the amusement of gossiping with any passing strangers. The sun rises. The boy fixes his eyes on a distant windmill, which seems to wave to him. He is puzzled because, at the turns of the road, the windmill appears on the left instead of the right. The day is hot and sullen.

The low hills were still plunged in the lilac distance, and no end could be seen to them. . . . But at last, when the sun was beginning to sink into the west, the steppe, the hills and the air could bear the oppression no longer, and, driven out of all patience, exhausted, tried to fling off the yoke. A fleecy ashen-grey cloud unexpectedly appeared behind the hills. It exchanged glances with the steppe, as though to say, "Here I am," and frowned. Suddenly something burst in the stagnant air; there was a violent squall of wind which whirled round and round, roaring and whistling over the steppe. At once a murmur rose from the grass and last year's dry herbage, the dust curled in spiral eddies over the road, raced over the steppe, and carrying with it straws, dragonflies and feathers, rose up in a whirling black column towards the sky and darkened the sun. Prickly uprooted plants ran stumbling and leaping in all directions over the steppe, and one of them got caught in the whirlwind, turned round and round like a bird, flew towards the sky, and turning into a little black speck, vanished from sight.

Then a corncrake is up, flying with the wind, not against it, not like the rooks "grown old in the steppe." Then "the cloud vanished, the sun-baked hills frowned and the air grew calm, and only somewhere the troubled lapwings wailed and lamented their destiny."

It irks us at first to see Chekhov personifying and moralizing nature in the romantic nineteenth-century way, but we know that a boy might very well do this. When night falls, "as though because the grass cannot see in the dark that it has grown old, a gay youthful twitter rises from it." Chekhov, the onetime chorister, hears the "whistling, scratching, the basses, tenors and sopranos of the steppe, all mingling in an incessant monotonous roar."

There is a haze; a solitary bush or boulder will look like a man. Such immobile waiting figures stand on the hills, hide behind the ancient barrows, peep out of the grass. The moon rises and the night grows pale and languid. The effect is eerie. The legends of the steppe come to the boy's mind, folktales told by some old nurse.

Up to now Chekhov is mostly evoking the steppe as the boy simply sees it. Presently, as in his short stories, Chekhov enters fully into the feelings of the boy he once was. The party has had a roadside meal, and while his elders sleep it off, the boy wanders about, hears someone singing one of those long plaintive, passionate songs, meaningless to a child. First of all, he thinks no one is there and that the grass is singing; then he suddenly sees that a woman is singing and this bores him, but now there is a startling sight. Another boy! He is standing nearby. The two boys stare at each other awkwardly, unbelieving, in a long silence, like two animals staring at their own kind. Suddenly Yegorushka calls, "What's your name?"

The stranger's cheeks puffed out more than ever; he pressed his back against the rock, opened his eyes wide, moved his lips and answered in a husky bass: "Tit!"

The boys said not another word to each other; after a brief silence, still keeping his eyes fixed on Yegorushka, the mysterious Tit kicked up one leg, felt with his heel for a niche and clambered up the rock; from that point he ascended to the next rock, staggering backwards and looking intently at Yegorushka as though afraid he might hit him from behind, and so made his way upwards till he disappeared altogether behind the crest of the hill.

The melancholy song has died away. Time drags on.

[To Yegorushka] it seemed as though a hundred years had passed since the morning. . . . God's world [had] come to a standstill. . . . with smarting eyes [he] looked before him; the lilac distance, which till then had been motionless, began heaving, and with the sky floated away into the distance. . . . It drew after it the brown grass, the sedge, and with extraordinary swiftness Yegorushka floated after the flying distance. Some force noiselessly drew him onwards, and . . . the wearisome song flew after in pursuit.

He comes out of his dream when Deniska, the driver, incurably boyish himself, distracts him by teaching him how to hop on one leg.

The narrative has scores of these little incidents. The most striking things are the encounters with people on the road. The priest is eager for gossip. The party arrive at a dirty inn run by an hysterically excited Jew and Solomon, his satanic and resentful brother. We remember that once when Chekhov was a boy he was rushed to such an inn when, after a swim, he collapsed with acute peritonitis, and a doctor saved his life. The young brother, Solomon, resents the older one because he had been treated as a servant in the past. Solomon's only moments of liberation have come to him when he had run off to do funny Jewish turns at local fairs, but at present he is all bitterness:

"What am I doing? . . . The same as everyone else. . . . I am my brother's servant; my brother's the servant of the visitors; the visitors are Varlamov's servants; and if I had ten millions, Varlamov would be my servant.

. . . because there isn't a gentleman . . . who isn't ready to lick the hand of a scabby Jew for the sake of making a kopeck. . . . Everybody looks at me as though I were a dog, but if I had money Varlamov would play the fool before me just as my brother Moysey does before you."

And he goes on to say: "I throw my money into the stove! . . . I don't want money, or land, or sheep."

Moysey says his brother is mad, never sleeps at night and is always thinking and thinking and when you ask him what he is thinking he is angry and laughs. They are all having tea, and Yegorushka is astounded to see Solomon counting his money, a huge pile of ruble notes. And then, as if in a dream, a beautiful and elegant woman comes in, a Polish countess with a huge estate, asking for the mysterious, powerful Varlamov; because she loves haggling in her deals with him, she laughs, doesn't mind if she is swindled. She is a legend for miles around. Everyone has fantastic stories of her wealth. Yegorushka will never forget that she kissed him, and he is left with the idea that the unseen Varlamov must be an all-powerful wonder. It is a blow to him later on when he at last sees the real Varlamov: he is a nondescript moneyed merchant who swanks about, giving orders to everyone.

The journey crawls on and suddenly the boy has a shock. They catch up with a long procession of wagons carrying wool, and the stern uncle calmly hands the scared boy over to a carter. The uncle has heard that the powerful Varlamov, with whom he and the priest are going to do a deal, has left the high road for a distant village. They will pick the boy up in a day or two. Now the boy is scared and alone. Still, the carters are a jolly lot. They stop to swim naked in a pool; they catch fish and tell frightening stories of robberies and murders.

And the boy finds for the first time in his life a real enemy—one of Chekhov's sinister and best-drawn characters, a bully named Dymov. He has heard the boy is being taken to "a gentleman's school" and treats him with provoking contempt. Dymov is the handsome son of well-to-do peasants but has run wild in his youth, spent his money and been forced to start at the bottom and become a laborer. He has dangerous fits of resentment and takes his resentment out on the boy. "You can't eat with your cap on, and you a gentleman, too!" he sneers. With no uncle or priest to protect him the boy faces a man he fears. He hates Dymov. In one of his sadistic fits Dymov sees a snake, jumps off his wagon and beats it to death, saying it is a viper. It is not; it is a harmless grass snake. To the carters and the boy this act is a terrible sin. Later on in his life Chekhov told the novelist Bunin that Dymov was the sort of déclassé who would either become a revolutionary or go to pieces—"but there will be no revolution in Russia."

Soon the sky puts on one of its grand scenes: an appalling thunderstorm—and evokes one of Chekhov's most famous descriptive images. There is a flash of lightning—"someone seemed to strike a match in the sky"—exactly the image a boy would use. The whole steppe is lit up, a hulking black cloud comes over, the wind tears the steppe to pieces, the thunder rolls across the sky. There is a downpour and the boy, alone in his wagon, covers himself with a straw mat and at one point sees a flash "so broad that [he] suddenly saw through a slit in the mat the whole highroad to the very horizon, all the waggoners and even Kiryukha's waistcoat."

The end of the story is flat, as life is for us when waking up from a long dream. Reality returns. His elders abruptly hand him over, at a cottage in a small town, to a woman who will take him to the school he dreads. The stern uncle and the jolly priest go off.

Some critics thought *The Steppe* was no more than a string of disconnected incidents; but the discerning saw it as a superb and sustained prose poem. If his reputation had been uncertain, now Chekhov is seen to be a master. The story at once appeared in one of the "thick journals"; he was awarded the Pushkin prize.

Chekhov also wrote other, shorter stories on comparable themes. One of these is *Happiness* (sometimes called *Fortune*). We are in the longer, secretive minds of the peasants and the shepherds. We can point to the exact incident in *The Steppe* from which *Happiness* was conjured. We see a shepherd sitting with others in the evening while the sheep are asleep and the dogs are quiet. The only sound is the talking of the men. Another figure (whom we have also briefly seen before) is a superior man, in fact the landowner's overseer, who stands listening with condescension to the folkish fancies of the shepherds, saying little beyond "Yes, it could happen." They are gossiping about a man called Yefim who was possessed of the Devil: it is claimed he had "whistling melons" in his "market garden" and a pike has been heard to laugh when it was caught by him; a shepherd says he has seem Yefim diguised as a "talking bullock." It is agreed that the Devil can make a rock whistle, for this was heard on the Day of Freedom when the serfs were liberated. And now the talkers are cunning enough to reveal other preoccupations with hearsay. Pretending to be stupid, they are testing the overseer. Is it true that there is treasure hidden in the steppe? Yefim had said so. He also said *he* had discovered it. They tell the dramatic story of the find and of how this clever man died without revealing where the treasure was hidden. We see the dream of Fortune—nevertheless, they ask, Is this happiness?—brought into the open. There is profit for everyone, but not for the peasants—is that not so?

The overseer gets on his horse and evades the question. He says, "Your elbow is near, but you can't bite it," and gallops off, leaving something in their minds never spoken of in the boundless steppe:

> The ancient barrows . . . had a sullen and death-like look; there was a feeling of endless time and utter indifference to man in their immobility and silence.

They know tales of all the treasure buried by generation after generation of robbers and Cossack invaders: Is that the real treasure?

The night goes on, the dawn begins. There is a sudden menacing sound racing over the steppe: "Tah! Tah! Tah! Tah!"—the sound of a bucket falling down a mine shaft. (We shall hear it years later in *The Cherry Orchard*, pronouncing the new industrial order that will ruin that feckless family.) The mines—they are the buried treasure! The industrial revolution is already destroying the grace and fertility of Nature. And *who* has the treasure? The gentry, the foreign immigrant miners, the government, all have it; not the shepherds.

Happiness has the note of fable, and its merit lies in the exact rendering of the shepherds' sly, wondering, legend-consuming talk as they interpret a new aspect of human fate. The ancient burial mounds of the steppe are monuments to races of men who have died, as all men and dispensations die. The drollery of the shepherds is a mask for longheaded thoughts. And one thing is historically important: Chekhov knows that shepherds are not *peasants*. As shepherds they are the last survivors of a nomadic culture and have an inherited earlier precivilized apprehension of human fate.

Chapter Six

In May 1888 Chekhov sent his brother Mikhail to the south to find a cottage which would house the "abnormal family" for the summer. Hearing their son's talk of the steppe, his parents longed for the scenes of their early years. The first reports were gloomy, but at last Mikhail found a place that was miraculously beautiful near Sumy on the Psyol River on the edge of the Ukraine. Anton wrote to Suvorin that it was delectable. Nightingales sang all day, he wrote. The countryside was a paradise of neglected gardens, sad and poetical estates shut up and deserted, where lived the souls of beautiful women, old footmen on the brink of the grave, young ladies longing for the most conventional love. It was a place that made one think of old novels and fairy tales. You could swim and fish in the river and angle for crayfish. A man for mysterious sounds, Chekhov heard the cry of the bittern for the first time, a cry that every Little Russian knew but none described the same way. It was partly the echoing blow on an empty barrel, partly the moo of a cow; but no one had even seen the bird!

The cottage was on the estate of the Lintvaryov family.

They were cultivated liberals in an old-fashioned way and gently reproved Chekhov for his ties with the conservative Suvorin. They were strict teetotalers. The mother was a kind, if flabby, old lady who adored old-fashioned poets and read Schopenhauer. Two of the daughters were doctors, one of them blind, epileptic and dying of a brain tumor, who laughed when Chekhov read some of his stories to her. Chekhov wrote:

> What seems strange to me is not that she is about to die, but that we do not feel our own death and write [stories] as though we would never die.

He went with the second daughter on her rounds to see her patients. She also managed the house and estate and knew all about horses. She was a tender doctor who suffered with her patients and Chekhov said he believed she had never hurt anyone, and "it seems to me that she never has been nor ever will be happy for a single minute." The third daughter was a vigorous girl with a loud voice, always laughing and singing, a passionate Little Russian patriot who had started schools in the village and taught the children there. There were two sons, one modest and hardworking—he had been sent down from the university for political reasons, "but of that he doesn't boast." The second son was mad about Tchaikovsky but had no talent. He admired the teachings of Tolstoy, though he could not stand Tolstoy's disciples. There were exploring trips in an ancestral four-in-hand carriage into the province of Poltava:

If you had only seen the place where we stayed the night and the villages stretching eight or ten versts through which we drove! What weddings we met on the road, what lovely music we heard in the evening stillness, and what a heavy smell of fresh hay there was!

He stayed for a night with a friend of the Lintvaryovs called Alexander Smagin, whom they nicknamed the Shah of Persia, in a crumbling and neglected house. The suckers of cherry and plum trees grew through the floorboards, and one night he saw a nightingale nesting between the window and the shutter and saw "little naked nightingales, looking like undressed Jew babies, hatched out from the eggs."

Chekhov went on to a literary pilgrimage through Gogol's country and came back with the astonishing idea of raising money for the founding of what he called a "climatic station" for writers. It would free them from the wasteful political quarrels of Moscow and Petersburg. Nothing came of this. On his return to Sumy there was trouble. Alexander's wife had died and he arrived with his children at the cottage. Alexander celebrated his arrival by escaping to the little town of Sumy and, in the public park, "assisting the performance of the local conjuror and hypnotist" by drinking and shouting foul language. He had to be dragged away. Worse, he had fallen in love with Yelena, one of the Lintvaryov sisters, and wanted to marry her. The girl might very well have been longing to marry but Chekhov sternly saw disaster. He knew his uncontrollable brother. After a serious row Alexander was packed off, protesting, to Petersburg: later he admitted he had been stupid to think of marrying her;

he had got used to living alone. In fact he found another lady and married her.

When high summer came Chekhov went to stay at Suvorin's house at Feodosiya in the Crimea. The journey to Sumy and then to Kharkov (he wrote to his sister) was dull, the Crimean steppe was as dull as the tundra, but he was enchanted by the ravines, they were superb, and he said they let his imagination work in tune with Gogol's story *A Terrible Vengeance*. Then he was in Sevastopol and saw the blue sea. At Feodosiya Suvorin talked too much: the subject was a play, *The Wood Demon*, which he wanted to write in co-operation with Chekhov. Feodosiya was a grayish, dreary little town, but the bathing was wonderful. On to the estate of Ivan Konstantinovich Ayvazovsky, a well-known marine painter who "is a combination of a general and a bishop . . . and a naïve grandfather and an Othello." He was a vigorous seventy-five-year-old and claimed to have known Pushkin but had never read him. "Why should I read," he said, "if I have my own opinions." After that Chekhov went on a dirty little cargo steamer called *Dir*. The sea was rough. The ship stank and during the night narrowly escaped a collision. He was seasick. A terrible night. The crew said the incompetent fat captain would wreck the ship, and the following year he did. Chekhov went on to ugly Batum, "a café-chantant sort of town," then on to Tiflis and Baku on the Caspian, "a rotten place," appallingly hot and stinking of kerosene, but he did see at last the superb sight of the famous Georgian Military Road, a road of "unbroken poetry, a wonderful, fantastic story written by Demon in love with Tamara."

Suvorin was repeating his warning not to hunt after two hares and urging Chekhov to give up medicine. Chekhov replied that if he did not have his medical work he doubted if he could give his leisure to literature. "There is no discipline in me." The "clinical" concern continues in the elaborate, long *The Birthday Party*, which follows Tolstoy's tedious habit of underlining what the characters speak with the very different thoughts they are harboring. Chekhov borrowed this manner because of his own obsession with what he called "lying," and in *The Birthday Party* he seems to be novelizing and moralizing rather than telling. We see a wife, oppressed by pregnancy, becoming jealous of her husband's habit of charming the ladies, and especially at his birthday party. The jealousy becomes a mania of dislike. He, too, has his hidden worry. Charming, all things to all men, he is nevertheless a bad-tempered judge, who is worried because his conduct at a trial is being challenged in the High Court. Chekhov follows the tension closely and begins well. The difficulty, he said, was to deal with the middle of the story, but here he is admirable. Nimbly he takes us through the wife's touchiness and snobbery at the party. Out in the exquisite garden there is a scene (cleverly taken from the scything scene in *Anna Karenina*) in which the self-important judge takes the scythe out of a young lady's hand and shows her how to use it as it should be used. And then, by a stroke of comic genius, the story "turns." A boating party is arranged. The husband jumps into the boat, causing it to "lurch violently," and takes charge. After sitting through the picnic on an island, the wife excuses herself and goes home in a carriage. That night her labor starts.

As a doctor, Chekhov was very proud of this scene, in which he records the mingling of jealousy and pain in the emotions of the woman. Ladies who read the story told him that he had exactly caught the emotional and physical sensations, the unreason and exhaustion, a woman feels. In the end the baby is stillborn and the husband and wife are facing a fact that calls them to account. When he read the story Suvorin was naïve enough to complain that Chekhov had not ended the story with the court scene, which the judge had yet to face.

In the following summer Chekhov took his family to the Lintvaryovs' estate once more. Nikolay had caught typhoid in Moscow and his tuberculosis was reaching its final stage. Anton nursed him day and night for weeks and was himself exhausted. He sent for Alexander—their quarrel had been made up—and then went off to stay with the Smagins once more to recover. He was no sooner there than a telegram came saying that Nikolay had died. After a terrible journey, changing trains at little junctions, Anton arrived in Sumy in time to join his brothers in carrying the body in an open coffin to the cemetery on the Ukrainian estate in the traditional manner of Ukrainian funerals. "We see people die," he had once said, "but do not think of our own death." He could not bear to stay at Sumy and did not know where to go or what to do.

"If there were faults in Nikolay's character," Anton said, "he has expiated them by his sufferings." And to Suvorin: "There's not a kopeck's worth of poetry left in life."

By chance an old school friend turned up: he was a cheerful fellow who had worked with Chekhov in *The Alarm*

Clock days. They went off to the handsome city of Odessa, on the Black Sea, where they found a group of young actresses from the Maly Theater in Moscow, who were on tour, and their frivolity distracted Chekhov. He was in and out of cafés and their rooms day and night.

"I practically wore skirts myself," he wrote to his brother Ivan, "and am living without thinking." He had spent nearly all his money. The girls tried to keep him, but when they saw he was determined to leave they gave him a couple of neckties—one of his minor vanities—and he left alone for one more tiring journey to "abominable Yalta."

Chapter Seven

Only writing, then, would purge his grief, but what would he write? He had wasted time at the Lintvaryovs. He started writing *A Dreary Story*, and it was to become one of the longest, strangest and most powerful and self-accusing stories of his "clinical" type. It is divided into six parts. The theme springs from a growing obsession which he had often discussed with Suvorin, and perhaps a chance meeting in Yalta brought it to a head. There was a colony of writers in the resort, and one morning Chekhov was stopped in the street by a bold young girl of fifteen who addressed him by name. She wanted him to read and criticize a tale she had written. Chekhov was one of the few writers who responded to such intrusions from women. He read the story, liked it and sent it to Suvorin, who published it. For a while he wrote, encouraging her, and then the acquaintance stopped.

But—to be addressed by a stranger by name in a strange town! He had found a subject: the price of fame is that one ceases in everyone's eyes, even in one's own, to be "an ordinary human being who *knows* he will die." This is the preoccupation of the famous professor of medicine in *A*

Dreary Story and indeed of Chekhov himself. (Moscow gossip said that the death of a professor in the medical school was the source. This seems to have been quite untrue.)

One is bound to think of *A Dreary Story* as a catharsis, even from the perversity of its title. It is a tour de force and an exemplar of the rule "When in doubt a writer should increase the difficulty." The twenty-nine-year-old Chekhov set himself the task of projecting himself into the intimate life of a learned man of sixty-two who has an incurable disease and knows he will soon die but has revealed nothing of this to his family and friends. He is a professor of medicine and celebrated throughout Russia and Europe. He is a member of all the Russian, and three European, universities. "All that and a great deal more," he writes, "makes up what is called my 'name.'" It is a matter of pride that his fame eclipses his life as an "ordinary human being." We see him writing a day-to-day diary, in the present tense and in the first person, looking back with rigid pride on his distinguished career and in the manner of a doctor recording his symptoms. Dryly—if with some vanity—he sets out his physical condition: a bald, dingy wrinkled old man with false teeth, mouth turning down at one side when he talks or lectures. He is subject to attacks of tic douloureux, the sight of which must stir "in everyone the grim and impressive thought, Evidently that man will soon die." His memory is going, his ideas now lack sequence; the simpler the subject he writes about, the more agonizing is the effort, and he feels more at ease writing a learned article than when composing a congratulatory letter or a memorandum. He notes that he writes better in German or English than in Russian.

Intellectually he is devastating. He knows he is unrepentantly an egotist. He still retains the belief

> that science is the most essential thing in the life of man; that it always has been and will be the highest manifestation of love. . . . This faith is perhaps naïve and may rest on false assumptions, but it is not my fault that I believe that and nothing else.

Although the voice in the story is exclusively the professor's, his "stream of consciousness" is as stern, sweeping and controlled as the Preacher's in the withering book of Ecclesiastes, yet the narrative is particular and rippling with the Chekhovian sense of intimate drama.

The professor is an insomniac. At night his household becomes clear to us because of the sounds made by his family.

> Two rooms away from me my daughter Liza says something rapidly in her sleep, or my wife crosses the drawing-room with a candle and invariably drops the matchbox; or a warped cupboard creaks.

An uneasy family. At dawn a cock crows, the porter below coughs with anger. The professor wakes and waits for his wife to come in and say—what she always says—that she is "just looking for something," before she asks how he has slept. He knows by heart what she will say. It will be about money: that he owes money to the porter; that he has forgotten to send the monthly fifty rubles to their son, who is leading an extravagant life in Warsaw; that bread (thank God) is cheaper, but sugar is going up; that their daughter Liza, who is studying at the conservatoire, is ashamed to go out in her shabby fur coat when everyone knows that her father is a professor of the highest distinction; and on to her nagging lament that he refuses to add to their income by going into private practice as a doctor. He tries to calm her. Liza comes in, looking as pretty as his wife used to look when she was young, but after his sleepless night it seems to him that her kiss is "like the sting of a bee. I give a false smile and turn my head away." Although he is a confirmed egotist he is ashamed of the secret thought that if his daughter were really concerned for him she would give up her expensive music lessons!

He is glad to be off to the university, to his real home, the home of his fame and power. Every day as he passes the little beer shop where, when he was a student, he used to make notes for his thesis, he never fails to remember dryly that this was where he wrote his first passionate love letters to his wife and that his thesis was entitled *Historia Morbi*. Now at the university he meets the old hall porter who knows by heart every item of the careers of a whole generation of professors; in his way, the porter is an unconscious parody of them. He has picked up a hundred words of Latin and makes "free use of our terminology" and is vain of being able to set up a skeleton for the lecturers. There is the comedy of the professor's interchanges with the faculty. They are all watching one another, of course; each of them obviously hoping to be his successor.

In Part Two he has returned home and is working in his

room within hearing of the chattering of his family. Presently he hears a discreet ring of the doorbell. He knows who has rung it. He hears the rustle of skirts and "a dear voice." It is the voice of Katya, his ward. He had taken her in to be brought up in the family when her father died eighteen years before. She had a small capital of her own. He remembers her as a trustful, apt and truthful little girl who used to sit quietly watching him as he worked. Everything went well until she was fourteen or so, when, as young girls do, she became stage-struck. They used to have long arguments about the theater. He has always hated the theater, especially the falsity of actors. Although he had done what he could to stop her, she suddenly joined a troupe of actors in Ufa or some such place. She had been wildly happy and wrote marvelous letters for four years, and then, of course, there was the usual disaster. She had fallen in love with an especially plausible actor, who soon left her. She had had a child by him and it died. She seems to have attempted suicide. The professor remembers that he wrote "boring" letters to her, sent her money, but he could no longer love her as he used to do.

That is all over. She has gone off now to live idly on her means in a flat nearby, an actressy place of cheap fans, silly pictures, little tables—all signs of spiritual scrappiness and indolence. Nevertheless, every day she drops in on the family, particularly to see *him*, and sits in his room watching him incuriously. To this ward of his he is a surrogate father. She is offhand with his wife and daughter, who have brought her up, and they have come to hate her. This hatred comes to a head when his daughter has a suitor. The professor is shocked by their hatred. It arouses his contempt for this primitive aspect of woman's feeling:

> I cannot recall one woman or girl of my acquaintance who would not consciously or unconsciously harbour such feelings. . . . Woman is as tearful and as coarse in her feelings now as she was in the Middle Ages and to my thinking [this is followed by the very Chekhovian view] those who advise that she should be educated like a man are quite right.

Now to farce. Enter his daughter's suitor. The professor is appalled by the ludicrous man, who now begins to dine with them again and again. Special expensive dishes are cooked for him; the finest wines are brought out. His name is Gnekker.

> He is . . . very stout and broad-shouldered, with red whiskers near his ears, and a little waxed moustache, which makes his plump smooth face look like a toy. He is dressed in a very short reefer jacket, a flowered waistcoat, breeches very full at the top and very narrow at the ankle, with a large check pattern on them, and yellow boots without heels. He has prominent eyes like a crab's, his cravat is like a crab's neck, and I even fancy there is a smell of crab-soup about the young man's whole person.

The professor himself reveals a primitive medieval tendency. Incredible, the professor thinks, that a daughter of his should love such an obvious fraud. And to think his wife is blind to it!

In Part Three the professor begins to spend more time with the grateful, watchful but foolish Katya, who has taken up with another professor, a clever, cynical philologist. The three play cards and drink. We become aware that the professor is jealous. What begins to strike us is that all the characters may be talking together but they are not listening: although close, they are fundamentally isolated, as if in separate rooms. This, of course, is common among the characters of all Chekhov's stories: they talk to one another but do not listen. We shall see this as being the spell of his plays later on in his life. In fact, *A Dreary Story* would indeed be a dreary if learned debate, but it has an unrepentant cold intellectual vivacity. In Part Five we have a burst of emotion in which all the parties break under the emotional strain and become clear to themselves.

In Part Six the professor goes alone to Kharkov to investigate Gnekker's background. The final scene is in his hotel room. He is "famous"—the newspapers have picked up the news that he, the celebrity, is there. No freedom for "an ordinary human being" who is famous! In three months perhaps the same paper will be reporting his death. He sits in his hotel room, alone in the dreary town. No one has heard of the Gnekker family. The man *is* a fraud. The next day the professer has a telegram from his wife saying that Gnekker and his daughter are married! There is a tap on the door of his hotel room. Enter Katya, who says she is traveling to the Caucasus and has discovered the hotel he is staying at. She says: "Help me! . . . I cannot go on. . . .

You are my father . . . my only friend! You are clever . . . you have lived so long; you have been a teacher!" In what will strike us for the first time as too obvious a trick on Chekhov's part she pulls a handkerchief out of her bag to wipe her tears and a bundle of letters falls out.

On one of them I recognize the handwriting of Mikhail [the philologist] and accidentally read a bit of a word: "passionat. . . ."

Clearly she is going to meet the philologist and this is her last appeal to the professor to tell her if she is right or wrong. In his account of this meeting the professor is powerless to make up his mind. He evades.

The absence of what my colleagues call a general idea I have detected in myself only just before death, in the decline of my days, while the soul of this poor girl has known and will know no refuge all her life, all her life!

All he can think of *doing* is to ask her to lunch. She recognizes the finality of his words and all he is able to think of saying is "Then, you won't be at my funeral?"

He watches her leave the room. The great "name" is powerless as a human being. He knows she has gone for good and he writes: "I've seen her black dress for the last time. . . . Farewell, my treasure!"

Many critics thought this story as remorselessly objective as Tolstoy's masterpiece *Ivan Ilyich*, about the great lawyer who knows he is dying. That resemblance is superficial.

There were minor criticisms. His friend Pleshcheyev said the professor ought to have said more about Katya's "husband." Chekhov replied that

> the professor could not write about Katya's husband because [she herself] does not say anything about him; besides one of my hero's chief characteristics is that he cares far too little about the inner life of those who surround him.

Many critics accused Chekhov of concealing, or at least being blind to, the unconscious erotic element in the relations of the old professor and Katya—a modern novelist would have made this central. Here Chekhov was indignant; if people, he wrote,

> lose belief in the friendship, respect and boundless love which exist outside the sphere of sex, at least they should not attribute bad taste to me. If Katya were in love with an old man barely alive you must agree it would be a sexual perversion. . . . If there had been nothing more than this sexual perversion, would it have been worthwhile to write the story?

Some complained that he had not given the professor's wife and daughter an inner life of their own, but Chekhov made the point that the egotistical professor was writing his own story and was absorbed in himself only and "had ceased to be sensitive to the family's feelings." In fact by masochistic indirection the professor has made us intimately aware of the family. Even in his anger about the "medievalism" of the mother and daughter we see that the professor is too self-centered to understand what is clear to us—that they are "ordinary human beings" who know their own minds, while he generalizes.

Of course the professor contains a good deal of Chekhov himself. The "lack of a central idea" haunted him as he wrote this intensely controlled story which projects so much of his own state of mind at this time. We notice how carefully his prose captures the professor's academic manner and how he sustains a moral diagnosis without losing the natural grace of the artist. The story is like some stern gravestone which records the public figure and in which at the same time, between the engraved lines, we detect the fitful human being. Under the surface of Chekhov's impressionism there is firm psychological architecture. After this story he will no longer be a moralizing Tolstoyan. As many critics have noticed, Chekhov is at the point of impasse. He has isolated himself.

Chapter Eight

SAKHALIN

Although friends of Chekhov had heard him say that he saw no difficulty in chasing two or even more hares at the same time, they were alarmed when, in 1890, the news leaked out that he was planning to travel across Russia and Asia to the Russian penal colony on the island of Sakhalin, Russia's notorious Botany Bay in the Far East. The nomad had been reborn. When he asked Suvorin to back him, Suvorin refused. That hare, Suvorin said, had died more than a generation ago. Even the story of *Manon Lescaut* was dead. Chekhov's duty was to literature, not to documentary investigation. And in any case, there was no trans-Siberian railway; the appalling land journey through barbarous country would kill him. Stirred by opposition and anxious to refute both his liberal and radical critics, who accused him of lacking "a general political idea," Chekhov fought back.

Sakhalin can be useless and uninteresting only to a society which does not exile thousands of people to it. . . . we have sent *millions* of men to rot in prison, have destroyed them—casually without thinking, barba-

rously . . . have depraved them, have multiplied criminals, and the blame for all this we have thrown upon
the gaolers and red-nosed superintendents. Now all educated Europe knows that it is not the superintendents
that are to blame, but all of us. . . . The vaunted [political
idealists of the] sixties did *nothing* for the sick and for
prisoners, so breaking the chief commandment of
Christian civilization.

When Mikhail Chekhov was asked what had put the idea
into his brother's head, he said it was an accident: Anton
had happened to read a penal document lying about in an
office. In Petersburg the gossip was that he wanted to go
in order to recover from an unhappy love affair with a married woman, Lydia Avilova, a sentimental novelist. This is
certainly untrue. After his death she wrote *Chekhov in My
Life*, which has been shown to be a wishful illusion. More
interestingly, when he had graduated as a doctor he had not
written his dissertation, and the desire to make amends by
writing a serious medical document that would qualify him
was strong. Indeed on his return from Sakhalin he did sub-
mit a manuscript to the university, where it was at once
rejected as unacademic.

There is no doubt that Chekhov felt he had the "duty of
repaying my debt to medicine." But it is very important also
that ever since his boyhood he had been a passionate reader
of the journeys of Przhevalsky, the greatest of Russian ex-
plorers, and had read Humboldt's journey across the steppe
and George Kennan's famous expedition to Siberia. More
intimately human are his words to a friend, the writer Ivan

Shcheglov, who supposed, naturally, that Chekhov was going simply to observe and "get impressions." Chekhov replied that he was going "simply to be able to live for half a year as I have not lived up to this time. Don't expect anything from me."

Suvorin gave in. Chekhov got his sister, his brother Alexander and friends to do exhaustive research for him in Petersburg. Among other responsibilities he had to see that his family had enough money to live on while he was away. He described his own state of excitement medically: "It's a form of lunacy: Mania Sakhalinosa."

He set off at last late in April 1890 on a four-thousand-mile journey that would last over three months. He had been spitting blood that winter. His sister and a few friends saw him off on the river steamer at Yaroslavl. He was equipped with a heavy leather coat and a short one, top boots, a bottle of cognac, a knife "useful for cutting sausages and killing tigers" and a revolver for protection against brigands—he never had to use it.

His account of his land and river journey is told in vivid letters to his sister and his mother.

The rain poured down during the river trip to the ravines of Kineshma. After leaving the steamer he took to the road, jolted in an open public coach from one posting house to the next, though he hired private carriages when he could, and sat there freezing "like a goldfinch in a cage."

He writes to his sister:

I have my fur coat on. My body is all right, but my feet are freezing. I wrap them in the leather overcoat,

but it is no use. I have two pairs of breeches on. . . .
Telegraph poles, pools, birch copses flash by. Here we
overtake some emigrants. . . . We meet tramps with
pots on their back; these gentry promenade all over
. . . Siberia without hindrance. One time they will murder some poor old woman to take her petticoat for their
leg-wrappers; at another they will strip from the verst
post the metal plate with the number on it—it might
be useful; at another will smash the head of some beggar
or knock out the eyes of some brother exile; but they
never touch travellers. . . .

He is by now well past the Urals. If the small towns are
gray and miserable, the country people are "good and
kindly," and

have excellent traditions. Their rooms are simply furnished but clean, with claims to luxury; the beds are
soft, all feather mattresses and big pillows. The floors
are painted or covered with homemade linen rugs.

No bugs, no "Russian smell." The explanation: these people
have forty-eight acres of black earth, which they farm
themselves.

But it cannot all be put down to prosperity. . . . One
must give some of the credit to their manner of life.
. . . they don't search in each other's heads in your
presence. . . . There is a cleanliness of which our Little
Russians can only dream, yet the Little Russians are far
and away cleaner than the Great Russians.

Food! Pies and pancakes are good, but all the rest is not for what Chekhov calls his "European" stomach. Duck broth is disgusting and muddy; there is the terrible "brick tea" tasting like a "decoction of sage and beetles."

The last of the bad Moscow air was out of his lungs and he had stopped coughing. But in Siberia there were freezing gales, food was scarce; the bad roads, the floods and the days and nights of jolting along brought on his cough again and he spat blood. He had bought a cart of his own by now because it was cheaper, but he was continually repairing it. His cheap boots cramped his feet and for the rest of the journey he suffered agonies from piles. His whole body was aching.

He changes to a public coach. It is like traveling on roads flooded to the size of lakes and he has to be rowed across them. As for fellow passengers—they seem chiefly to have been drunkards and boasters. There was a police officer who had written a play and insisted on reading it. He also exhibited a nugget of gold. There was constant talk about gold in Siberia.

Tomsk turns out to be a dull and drunken town—"a pig in a skullcap" and the acme of "mauvais ton." It is regarded as a distinction that all its governors die in it.

After the freezing gales the heat of summer comes suddenly. He had his first bath at Irkutsk, "a very European town," and threw away his filthy clothes and bought new ones. Then on by river steamer to the famous Lake Baikal, a little sea in itself, and at last he reached a paradise on the Amur River. On the left, the Russian shore; on the right, wild and deserted China. What a region for a summer villa, among duck, grebes, herons and all sorts of creatures with long beaks, young girls smoking cigarettes, old ladies smoking pipes. Marvelous crags and forests, everyone talking about gold, gold, gold.

And what liberalism! Oh what liberalism. . . . People are not afraid to talk aloud here. There's no one to arrest them and nowhere to exile them to, so you can be as liberal as you like. The people for the most part are independent, self-reliant and logical. If there is any misunderstanding at Ustkara, where the convicts work (among them many politicals who don't work), all the Amur region is in revolt. . . . An escaped convict can travel freely on the steamer to the ocean, without any fear of the captain's giving him up. This is partly due to the absolute indifference to everything that is done in Russia.

At last, after two and a half months, on July 5, 1890, he is at Nikolayevsk, a town of respectable smugglers on the Tatar Strait and the port of embarkation for the island of Sakhalin on the other side of the strait. On the crossing he found himself with three hundred soldiers and several prisoners, one he notices "accompanied by his five-year-old daughter, who clung to his shackles as he came up the gangway."

The first sight of the town itself alarmed him. Smoke was drifting across the strait from huge fires. He eventually wrote in *The Island: A Journey to Sakhalin*:

The horrifying scene, compounded of darkness, the silhouettes of mountains, smoke, flames and fiery sparks, was fantastic. On my left monstrous fires were burning, above them the mountains, and beyond the mountains a red glow rose to the sky from remote conflagrations. It seemed that all of Sakhalin was on fire.

Chekhov had had no difficulty in getting permission to talk to the convicts or the settlers, but his official permit forbade him to talk with political prisoners. He had given practical forethought to his inquiry and he had shrewdly decided to begin by making his personal census of the population. He devised a card of twelve questons, which requested simple particulars of each settler's status, age, religion, education and year of arrival, and included the very cogent question: Married in Russia or in Sakhalin? He claimed to have filled out ten thousand of those cards. There was no Impressionist in Chekhov, the doctor. Most of the settlers were of peasant origin and illiterate. Some didn't know where they came from. There were twice as many men as women in the penal colony, and in addition there were the "bachelor soldiers," who were as dangerous, he noted, as "roughnecks building a railroad" near a Russian village.

If he is writing a flat documentary prose and rather overloads his book with the statistics, he has the storyteller's eye for the grim and the bizarre. When word of a new delivery of woman convicts gets around, we shall see, the road is crowded with men going south to the port of arrival. These are known to everyone, not without irony, as the "suitors," or prospective bridegrooms.

They actually look like bridegrooms. One has donned a red bunting shirt, another wears a curious planter's hat, a third sports shining new high-heeled boots, though nobody knows where he bought them or under what circumstances. When they arrive at the post they are permitted to enter the women's barracks and they are left there with the women. The suitors wander around the plank beds, silently and seriously eyeing the women; the latter sit with downcast eyes. Each man makes his choice. Without any grimaces, without any sneers, very seriously, they act with humanity toward the ugly, the old and those with criminal features. . . . If some younger or older woman "reveals herself" to a man, he sits down beside her and begins a sincere conversation. She asks if he owns a samovar and whether his hut is covered with planks or straw. . . . Only after the housekeeping examination has been completed, when both feel that a deal has been made, does she venture to say: "You won't hurt me in any way, will you?"

The conversation is over. The civil marriage is completed and he takes his "cohabitant" home.

With the exception of women from the privileged classes or those who arrived with their husbands, all female convicts became "cohabitants." Most of the women convicts were neurotics who had been "sentenced for crimes of passion or crimes connected with their families." They say, "I came because of my husband," or "I came because of my mother-in-law."

Most are murderers, the victims of love and family despotism. Even those who are sent out here for arson and for counterfeiting are being punished for their love affairs, since they were enticed into crime by their lovers.

Now they were "settled." Twenty years before Chekhov's time such women were sent to brothels.

Chekhov made a study of the grim mining settlements all over the island. Due was a place of violent brawls and robberies. On another journey there is a place called Upper Armudan, famous for its cardplayers. They gambled here with their rations and clothing. Once he was obliged to stay in a garret in the jail because the only other room was fully occupied by bugs and cockroaches. The jailer said these creatures "win all the time."

It seemed as though the walls and ceiling were covered with black crepe, which stirred as if blown by a wind. From the rapid and disorderly movements of portions of the crepe you could guess the composition of this boiling, seething mass.

During his journeys Chekhov came across dozens of criminal life stories. He got used to the apathy of the women, but the lot of the children born there horrified him.

What is terrifying in the cities and villages of Russia is commonplace here. . . . When children see chained convicts dragging a wheelbarrow full of sand, they hang onto the back of the barrow and laugh uproariously.

They played Soldiers-and-Convicts and Vagrants among themselves and knew the exact meaning of "executioner," "prisoners in chains," and "cohabitant." He records a talk with a boy of ten.

"What is your father's name?" I asked him.

"I don't know," he answered. . . .

"You are living with your father and don't know his name? That is disgraceful."

"He's not my real father."

"What do you mean, he's not your real father?"

"He's my mother's cohabitant."

"Is your mother married or a widow?"

"A widow. She came because of her husband."

"What do you mean, she came because of her husband?"

"She killed him."

In spite of this Chekhov was convinced that the children were "the most useful, the most necessary and the most pleasant" creatures on the island and that the convicts themselves felt this too. The children loved their "impure mothers and criminal fathers more than anything else in the world. . . . often children are the only tie that binds men and women to life, saving them from despair and a final disintegration." Yet the parents seemed indifferent to child prostitution.

The most horrifying pages of the book are those describing a flogging. Chekhov steeled himself to watch it and to record almost every stroke and all the screams of the criminal and the cold professional attitude of the flogger, counting out the strokes. Chekhov was impelled to identify himself with all the pain on the island. The one relief from the sight of human degradation came to him from the sights of nature: the crops, the forests, the animals, birds and shoals of fish. He studied the agriculture of the island very seriously. Writing the book when he was back home was a trying labor for one who was not by nature a documentary journalist. He added very enlightening footnotes. The book did not appear until 1895.

By October he was glad to leave Sakhalin, glad to stop being a doctor, examining human degradation, and to be a free globe-trotter. He left on a steamer by way of Hong Kong and Singapore. He reveled above all in Ceylon, where, he claimed in a letter to Alexander, he had made love to a dark girl under the palm trees; he also acquired three mongooses, and then went on to Odessa. At Tula his mother and sister met him, and then home to Moscow. He had been away eight months. He was thirty. He told his friends and family:

I can say I have lived! I've had everything I want. I have been in Hell which is Sakhalin and in Paradise which is Ceylon.

He was restless. This labor of writing a "book of statistics" hung over him like a punishment for a long time, for once more he was frantic about money. He had spent more than he could afford. His mind was full of stories begging to be written.

The man so conscientious in his duties inevitably craved

once more for escape and evasion. The "cure" was more travel and, although protesting, he jumped recklessly at the chance of a trip to Europe with Suvorin. The distraction was indeed a cure. On Sakhalin he had simply worked too hard; now with Suvorin and Suvorin's son he moved from barbarism to civilization. Vienna amazed him. He had never seen anything like this in his life.

> I have for the first time realized. . . . that architecture is an art. And here the art is not seen in little bits, as with us, but stretches over several miles. And then on every side street there is sure to be a bookshop. . . . It is strange that here one is free to read anything and to say what one likes.

They went on to Venice: "For us poor and oppressed Russians it is easy to go out of our minds here in a world of beauty, wealth, and freedom," he writes. And in another letter: "And the house where Desdemona lived is to let!"

On they went to Bologna and Florence. What works of art! What singing! What neckties in the shops! In Naples he was enchanted by the famous aquarium and studied the grace and viciousness of the exotic fish. He climbed Vesuvius and looked down on the crater and heard "Satan snoring under cover of the smoke." In Monte Carlo he could not resist a gamble and lost more than he could afford. "If I had money to spare I would spend the whole year gambling"— and, in one sense, his own life had become a gamble. In Nice he thought the luxury of the resort vulgarized the scenery. In Paris there were riots, but he thought the French "magnificent." He was impressed at the Chamber of Deputies, where he heard a free and stormy debate on the behavior of the police in the riots. Imagine the freedom to criticize the police! For once in his life he was staying in luxury hotels. He loved the Moulin Rouge but he eventually tired of "men who tie boa constrictors round their bodies, ladies who kick up to the ceiling, flying people, lions, *cafés chantants*, dinners and lunches." He wanted to get back to work. His depression had gone.

On Mondays, Tuesdays and Wednesdays I write my Sakhalin book, on the other days, except Sunday, my novel, and on Sundays, short stories.

He had paid his debt to medicine.

Chapter Nine

The immediate reward of Chekhov's Sakhalin adventure was an extraordinary leap of his imagination. It was prompted by an incident he had witnessed on the sea voyage home. He had seen two men buried at sea. In *Gusev* he turns from his prison documents to a fable that grows out of this incident and, one must suppose, from his preoccupation with his own illness. Gusev is traveling by sea with other soldiers sent home on sick leave. They are on edge and their talk is querulous and wanders between their real life of the moment and delirium. At sea one simply exists, outside society. Three soldiers are playing cards, and one of them drops his cards in the middle of the game and lies down on the floor. Dryly and offhand the others realize he has died. We listen to Pavel, a townsman, who is angered by his fears: his pain has made him sadistic. He is a class-conscious political, a real recalcitrant, who hates the officer class: he is contemptuous and patronizing of the naïve Gusev, who is a peasant. Pavel jeers at Gusev, telling him that he won't last the voyage; he is an ignorant peasant anyway. For example, Gusev believes what some soldier had told him: that in the night a big fish had collided with the ship and made a hole in it. When the wind howls Gusev believes that "the wind has broken loose from its chain." Pavel mocks him. To Gusev's peasant imagination images are facts. He says:

> "Suppose the fish were as big as a mountain and its back were as hard as a sturgeon and, in the same way, supposing that away yonder at the end of the world there stood great stone walls and the fierce winds were chained up to the walls."

Tiring of that fancy, Gusev's fevered mind drifts to precise visions of his home, and he sees his little daughter come out on her sleigh wearing big felt boots, and then, in terror, he sees

> a huge bull's head without eyes, and the horse and sledge are not driving along, but are whirling round and round in a cloud of smoke. But still he was glad he had seen his own folks.

Pavel grouses about the injustices that have been done to him and boasts of how clever he had been in tricking officials into thinking he is a man of superior class. "I am a living protest," he says. Pavel carries on with his sneers and his rage. He is going back to Russia to defy everyone: "That is what one can call life." It is Pavel who dies next. Days later Gusev dies. Orderlies wrap up the bodies in a sailcloth and manhandle these human parcels. We see Gusev's body somersaulting into the sea.

Here the imagination of Chekhov himself breaks into the story, which has become a poetic allegory. We remember that he had allowed the boy's imagination to take over scenes in *The Steppe*. Now Chekhov becomes the dead body of Gusev hitting the sea when he is buried.

After sinking sixty or seventy feet, he began moving more and more slowly, swaying rhythmically, as though he were hesitating. . . . Then he was met by a shoal of the fish called harbour pilots. . . . After that another dark body appeared. It was a shark. It swam under Gusev with dignity and no show of interest, as though it did not notice him, and sank down upon its back, then it turned belly upwards and languidly opened its jaws with two rows of teeth. The harbour pilots are delighted, they stop to see what will come next. After playing a little with the body the shark nonchalantly puts its jaws under it, cautiously touches it with its teeth, and the sailcloth is rent its full length from head to foot; one of the weights falls out and frightens the harbour pilots, and striking the shark on the ribs goes rapidly to the bottom.

At the very end of the story Chekhov turns our eyes away to the relieving presence of the evening sky, to evening clouds changing shape and color as the sun sinks. One will take the shape of a lion, another a triumphal arch, a third cruelly like a pair of scissors. More strangely, there is a moment when a cold green light shoots across the sky at the day's beginning and again at its end—an earthly yet strangely unearthly message of birth and death, a signal: Nature is "other."

At first reading the underwater scene seems to be an escape into the bizarre and breaks with the tone of the story: perhaps it was introduced because Chekhov himself, during his voyage home, could not resist swimming! He was tied to the ship by a rope, in the shark-infested Indian Ocean. On second thoughts we see that the whole story is a visionary meditation on the helpless "holiness of the human body," and we see also that the incident is entirely written in the same key as the talk of Pavel and Gusev: they are sick, they are delirious. Pavel's boastings of his political wrongs and his angry conviction of his superiority are as much fantasy as is Gusev's peasant vision of the bull's head and his belief that a fish can make a hole in the ship and that the winds are breaking out of walls to which they are chained. Chekhov's imagination seems to be transforming and allaying his own fears in his race with death. The realist is for the moment a Symbolist.

The more lasting influence of Sakhalin was that the convicts and settlers had given him an intimate and grimmer knowledge of peasant life in Russia—where 80 percent of the population were peasants. *Peasant Wives* is plainly a Sakhalin story. Crime grows out of the family quarrels of the peasants, quarrels of greed, jealousy and adultery in which the women, especially, brood on the killings they urge the men to do. Their talk tells all.

The married Varvara is sleeping with the priest's son for half a ruble a time, but she tells another woman:

"[It's] better to be struck dead by thunder than live like this. I'm young and strong and I've a filthy crooked hunchback for a husband, worse than Dyudya himself, curse him! When I was a girl, I hadn't bread to eat, or a shoe to my foot, and to get away from that wretchedness I was tempted by Alyoshka's money, and got caught like a fish in a net, and I'd rather have a viper for my bedfellow than that scurvy Alyoshka. . . . You work like a horse and never hear a kind word. . . . I'd rather beg my bread, or throw myself into the well."

The two women lie down to sleep in the yard and talk about young Mashenka, who poisoned her husband and died in jail.

"I'd make away with my Alyoshka and never regret it," Varvara says softly.

"You talk nonsense, God forgive you."

Varvara whispers: "Let us get rid of Dyudya and Alyoshka."

"God would chastise us."

"Well, let Him."

So thoughts of murder creep into the next day. The sunrise lights up the crosses in the churchyard and the next moment the sun is flashing on the windows, the sheep have got loose and peasant women are shouting at the shepherd, who is playing his pipes and pauses to crack his whip. What had been a woman's raw and short confession in Sakhalin Chekhov has domesticated in the working life of any Russian day. Mashenka had poisoned her husband after he had thrashed her with a bridle. He had walked with her in the chain gang after her trial. Their forgotten life comes to us as we listen to the two women's whispering.

Another story whose roots can be traced to Sakhalin is the extraordinary, violent *Murder*, written four years later in 1895, in which we find a wretched, religious hypocrite— a character who recalls the peasant hypocrite Iudushka, who appears in Shchedrin's *The Golovlyov Family*.

While Chekhov was still working on and off on the Sakhalin book—and indeed while he continued his research for it—he was writing stories to "keep my family from starving"; to pay off the debts he had run into in his travels. He continued to run after two hares—literature and what had become social medicine. There was famine among the peasants in many provinces, and he put down his pen to collect subscriptions for its relief, and went to the scene. In *The Wife*, a story that has been underrated by many critics, there is an account of a landowner being forced by his wife against his will to collect relief. He drives wildly by sleigh through the stricken villages and achieves nothing beyond a night of gluttony.

Before Sakhalin Chekhov had been strangely carried away by Tolstoy's *Kreutzer Sonata*. Now he begins to change his mind about Tolstoy:

Something in me protests. . . . reason and justice tell me that in the electricity and heat of love for man there is something greater than chastity and abstinence from meat. War is an evil and legal justice is an evil; but it does not follow that I ought to wear bark shoes and sleep on the stove with the labourer and so on. . . . But that is not the point, it is not a matter of pro and con; the thing is that . . . Tolstoy has passed for me, he is not in my soul, and he has departed from me, saying: "I leave this your house empty." I am untenanted. I am sick of theorising of all sorts. . . . Patients in a fever do not want food, but they do want something, and that vague craving they express as "longing for something sour. . . ." I, too, want something sour. . . . I notice the same mood in others. . . . It is as if they had been in love, had fallen out of love . . . and now were looking for some new distraction. . . . Natural science is performing miracles now.

Natural science! In *The Duel* we see the conflict between Tolstoy's Christian ethic and Darwinism and a reply to the accusation that Chekhov had evaded the crucial Russian demand for a statement of his "convictions." In his letters he calls *The Duel* a novel. It is not episodic and haphazard like the discarded *Stories of the Lives of My Friends*, but a long, carefully designed piece of work held together by a central conflict of ideas sustained to the end and rooted in the interplay of the characters and the influences of the scene. It is one of his most sustained yet various and discreetly ordered fictions. It seems to have been provoked by a meeting with a German zoologist, a strong Darwinian and a dogmatic believer in the survival of the fittest. In the story Chekhov describes a zoologist, Von Koren, who happens to be staying briefly at a Caucasian seaside resort before setting out on a scientific expedition to the Bering Strait.

In the resort he passes the time with an idle hospitable doctor, studies the guests and decides that one of them, Layevsky, is a decadent and irresponsible Petersburg type whom Nature will reject as unfit to survive. If the Layevskys of this world are not disposed of they will corrupt and destroy civilization. They are vain, they are loose in their morals, they corrupt women, they are irresponsible and idle. The mere sight of Layevsky wandering about the town in his slippers, playing cards all night and talking about himself and his ideals, condemns him in Von Koren's eyes.

And indeed, in one of the most original ironical opening scenes Chekhov ever wrote, we see Layevsky at his most lamentable. He and the amiable doctor—one of Chekhov's skeptics who are ashamed of their good nature—have gone to the beach to take a morning dip and are up to their shoulders in water. The secretive Layevsky has chosen this moment to ask the doctor's advice: "Suppose you had loved a woman and had been living with her for two or three years, and then left off caring for her, as one does, and began to feel that you had nothing in common with her. How would you behave in that case?" Just tell her to go where she pleases, says the doctor. But suppose, says Layevsky, she has no friends to go to, no money, no work. Five hundred rubles down or an allowance of twenty-five a month, the doctor says. Nothing more simple. But, Layevsky says, even supposing you have five hundred rubles and the woman is educated and proud, *how* would you do it?

Samoylenko was going to answer, but at that moment a big wave covered them both, then broke on the beach and rolled back noisily over the shingle. The friends got out and began dressing. "Of course, it is difficult to live with a woman if you don't love her," said Samoylenko, shaking the sand out of his boots. "But one must look at the thing humanely, Vanya. If it were my case, I would never show a sign that I did not love her, and I should go on living with her till I died." He was at once ashamed of his own words; he pulled himself up and said: "But for aught I care, there might be no females at all. Let them all go to the devil."

Layevsky nags away shamelessly. He is one of those "superfluous men of the sixties"—we have seen the type in *On the Road* and in *Ivanov*. "I have to generalize about everything I do," Layevsky continues. "Last night, for example, I comforted myself by thinking all the time: Ah, how true Tolstoy is, how mercilessly true!" He had run away with a married woman to live an idyll, the simple life in the Caucasus, but now they are quarreling. The house smells of ironing, powder, medicine. The same curling irons are lying about every morning. The doctor says: "You can't get on in the house without an iron," and blushes at Layevsky speaking "so openly of a lady he knew."

There is no hotel in the little resort. The doctor, who loves his food, runs a little table d'hôte where he entertains his friends, who include a silly young deacon who is Von Koren's butt because he will talk of nothing but religion. The deacon's only resource is liability to accident, a matter of importance to the story later on.

We now see Nadezhda Fyodorovna at home. She has no

idea that Layevsky is plotting to leave her. She is absorbed
in her restlessness. She has been unable to resist going to
bed with a vulgar police officer in the town and is also being
tempted by the son of a shopkeeper to whom she owes
money for her gaudy dresses. She knows she cannot control
her sexuality. *The Duel* is one of the rare Chekhov stories
in which the sexual subject is explicit. Her state is activated
by an intimate illness.

> She was glad that of late Layevsky had been cold to
> her, reserved and polite, and at times even harsh and
> rude; in the past she had met all his outbursts, all
> his contemptuous, cold or strange incomprehensible
> glances, with tears, reproaches, and threats to leave him
> or starve herself to death; now she only blushed, looked
> guiltily at him, and was glad he was not affectionate to
> her. If he had abused her, or threatened her, it would
> have been better and pleasanter, since she felt hopelessly
> guilty towards him.

In her kitchen she flushes "crimson" when she looks at her
cook, as though fearing the cook might hear her thoughts.

In another beach scene we see her sharing a bathing hut
with a deeply respectable married woman. Later, after Nadezhda's husband has died, this woman will tell her that it
is her duty to society to marry Layevsky at once, and will
refer to the state of Nadezhda's underclothes—emblems of
sin—which she has seen at the beach. She cannot allow her
children to come near her. Nadezhda is naïvely incredulous.
While she lies in bed all day, Layevsky, who has a minor

and neglected job in the Civil Service, is out all day and night on secretive journeys, intriguing to get the doctor to lend him money or to raise it from his friends, so that he can leave his mistress and go to Moscow.

We notice that Chekhov has the art of building his stories out of small journeys that lead to longer and more decisive journeys, in which his people gather together and then redistribute themselves and unknowingly create the stages of their fate. In *The Duel* the picnic scene is one of the most impressive examples of this art. His people drive in coaches to a gorge in the wild mountains where all will have the sensation that Nature has shut them in. As if a chorus, silent peasants, perhaps alien Tatars, will creep out and watch the picnic as polite Samoylenko lights a fire and fusses over cooking a meal. The tourists wander about and Layevsky provokes an argument with Von Koren. Later, Von Koren talks of Layevsky and Nadezhda as a pair of immoral brainless Japanese monkeys. She is wandering gaily off, followed by her ex-lover, the coarse police captain, whom she is ashamed of, and now snubs. He works himself up into a stage speech: "And so it seems our love has withered before it has blossomed, so to speak," and sulks off. She is now approached by a beach acquaintance, the dandyish son of a rich shopkeeper, and is surprised to find herself thinking that she could easily get her large debt to him wiped out if she agreed to go to bed with him. It would be fun to do that and then send him packing.

The peasants, sitting apart in the darkness, start quietly singing, and this stirs the naïve deacon and sends his mind traveling in the dream that in ten years' time he will be a holy archimandrite, leading beautiful religious processions in his uncle's church. At midnight the party will return quarreling, each frantic to pursue a secret dream. Nadezhda will be forced to give in to the police captain once more; his rival, the shopkeeper's son, will take his revenge and in a very dramatic night scene will take Layevsky to the low house of rendezvous, where he will be convinced of his mistress's guilt. Layevsky will have an attack of hysteria and accuse the doctor and Von Koren of "spying" on him and will fling at them a challenge to a duel. Firmly the challenge is accepted by Von Koren; he has been itching for it.

Chekhov is dramatic, but never melodramatic. Once more the rippling details of the journeys of the mind disperse melodrama. He has an instinct for the musical interweaving of changing moods. It is perfect that the duel is at dawn, at the remote, innocent scene of the picnic, where the morning landscape is changed after a stormy night. We see the foolish deacon, frightened and yet unable to resist the deplorable sight of a duel. In his way the deacon is a comic, calming, diversionary character, born to lose the thread of his ideas, but he is delightful in his naïve curiosity, which saves him from his doubts: though duelists are heathens and an ecclesiastical person "should keep clear of their company," was it just to shun them?

"They are sure to be saved," he says aloud, lighting a cigarette. "Human life," he reflects, "is so artlessly constructed. . . ." He compromises, when he arrives at the scene, by hiding in a field to watch.

How does Chekhov evoke the first sign of daylight? By a simple, strange detail: the deacon knows that daylight has come because he can at last see the white stick he is carrying.

The duel itself is amateurish. Von Koren has brought two young officers as seconds; they have never been present at a duel and bicker comically about the formalities. Is this the moment to propose a reconciliation? There is a doctor, who is careful to demand his fee. Layevsky is certain, as he stares at Von Koren, that the man intends to kill him. A second before Von Koren fires the deacon jumps up in the maize field and shouts and the shot faintly grazes Layevsky's neck.

To later critics the final act of the story is spoiled by its moral ending in the Tolstoyan fashion, for the lovers forgive each other. This is, however, very convincing. Layevsky has had a fright and gets down seriously to work in order to pay his debts. He and his mistress move into a humbler house. We hear no more of the minor characters, who have played their part in the indispensable chorus. On second thoughts we see the end is open, even after the reconciliation, which embarrasses the two enemies. Layevsky eagerly goes to see his enemy off at the harbor. Von Koren is rowed out to the steamer that will take him on his expedition. The sea is very rough. Born to dramatize and moralize about his situation, Layevsky watches the boat driven back by the waves yet, in the end, strongly making progress. He thinks:

So it is in life . . . in the search for truth man makes two steps forward and one step back. . . . And who knows? Perhaps they will reach the real truth at last.

Chekhov took great trouble with the last lines of his stories. Here he is dryly dismissive:

It began to spot with rain.

The strength of *The Duel* lies in the ingenuity of its playlike architecture, in which the major characters make speeches and the minor characters act as a chorus. They are not a passive moralizing chorus—they incite the action. The Tatar onlookers watch almost in silence. To them the imbroglio is alien. If, as everyone has noticed, Tolstoy's influence is still marked, Chekhov is more forgiving of Nadezhda's sexual misdemeanor than Tolstoy is of the wife in *The Kreutzer Sonata*. Reserve rather than abstinence, pity rather than condemnation, are more characteristic of Chekhov.

While he was deep in the elaborate design of *The Duel* and still laboring over his documentary book on Sakhalin, he could rely on his virtuosity to write satirically of an adultery in *The Grasshopper*. It is very sternly a Tolstoyan story; indeed Tolstoy admired it as a parable on "the wages of sin." We see a giddy young wife, married to a doctor who is dedicated to his profession, having a secret affair with a painter whom she has drawn to her silly "artistic" salon. She is soon disillusioned when the painter takes her to live among an art colony in the country. The painter drops her and she returns to her husband, a shy and saintly man, who pretends not to know. This, at the center of the story, is ingeniously managed. Accident intervenes: the doctor catches a fatal infection at his hospital and dies. The wife is frantic with remorse. How to convey her remorse at a deathbed? Here Chekhov, the doctor, is masterly. Her head is full of noises of the house as the doctors try to save her husband. She hears the monotonous striking of the clock, hour after hour, and the sound grows into a dull roar. She sinks into a doze on her bed.

> She dreamed that the whole flat was filled from floor to ceiling with a huge piece of iron and that if they could only get the iron out they would all be light-hearted and happy. Waking she realized that it was not the iron but Dymov's illness that was weighing on her.
> Nature morte, port . . . she thought, sinking into forgetfulness again. Sport—Kurort . . . and what of Shrek? Shrek . . . trek—wreck. . . . And where are my friends now? . . .

Her lover, the fashionable painter, had the silly boring habit of making up nonsensical, rhyming words that used to amuse her: now they are part of her torture.

And again the iron was there.

How close to the images and sounds, frightening and then puerile, Chekhov comes.

Too close, in fact. Making up silly rhyming words was a mannerism of his friend the painter Levitan, who was enraged and threatened a libel action. He was a well-known fantasist and suicidal neurotic. However, the quarrel passed off.

Chapter Ten

In 1891 Chekhov was living under great strain. He was unable to take his family to the Lintvaryov estate in the Ukraine because the doctor-daughter of the family, the woman with the tumor on the brain, had died. Chekhov's father, Pavel, had retired from his ill-paid job at the haberdashery warehouse and now plagued the home and raged against his wife. Chekhov did at last find a house for the summer months at Bogimovo, a huge mansion in which the family occupied only the top floor, but it was annoying that the rest of the house had been sublet. He was still grinding away at the now uncongenial and long documentary study of Sakhalin. He got up at five in the morning to toil on *Sakhalin* on Mondays, Tuesdays and Wednesdays. The rest of the week he worked on stories.

I dream of winning forty thousand [rubles], so as to cut myself off completely from writing, which I am sick of, to buy a little bit of land and live . . . in . . . seclusion.

And then comes news of famine in Nizhny Novgorod. The crops had failed and the peasants were killing their horses. He stopped writing and for months gave himself solely to the national appeal for funds to save the farmers. He traveled about begging money—helped by Suvorin—from the rich landowners and exhausted himself. By the winter he had a long bout of influenza; his secret illness was now attacking his stomach and bowels. It was clear that he could not stay in Moscow. He must get a house of his own in the country. In the early spring he heard of one in the village of Meli-khovo in the Serpukhov district, two hours away from Moscow by train. A painter was selling up and, typically, Chekhov was sure of the house before he saw it. It was more than a house. Five hundred and seventy-five acres of land went with it. The "son of a serf" was fulfilling a secret dream: he was setting up as a landowner himself with an estate! There was a park, a fruit garden, a long avenue of limes. Chekhov borrowed four thousand rubles from Suvorin and got a ten-year mortgage: the total cost was thirteen thousand rubles. If he had been in Germany, he said, he would certainly have been made a duke! The land was divided into two plots, one hundred acres being woodland and copse:

The barns and sheds have been recently built, and have a fairly presentable appearance. The poultry house is made in accordance with the latest deductions of science, the well has an iron pump. The whole place is shut off from the world by a fence in the style of a palisade.

The roof of the house was of corrugated iron, there was "a verandah, French windows, and so on," but the house was "not sufficiently new, having outside a very stupid and naïve appearance, and inside swarms with bugs and beetles."

There was the indispensable pond full of carp and tench, and a stream. The family moved in and slaved for months at putting the house to rights. One amusing effect of the move was that old Pavel's choleric temper calmed down. It was he, indeed, the real "son of a serf," who at once gave himself the airs of an aristocratic landowner, who insisted on being called Master by the peasants and servants and restored dignity to the village by organizing the Easter singing at the church. The peasants were delighted to have a doctor in residence for the first time in their lives and Chekhov soon had a thousand patients trooping to the door. "A nice man," one said. "He gives me medicine and doesn't charge me anything." Labor was cheap: "I begin to see the charms of capitalism," Chekhov said.

Mice swarmed in the house. Chekhov trapped them and went out into the woods to set them free. He loathed killing animals and had given up shooting years before. His sister gave up her art classes in Moscow, and they were soon out planting hundreds of trees and she managed the large kitchen gardens. In the first year there were "mountains of cucumbers, marvelous cabbages," and the corn harvest was excellent. The disasters were enjoyable:

Our gander [Chekhov wrote to his friends in the South] jumped on the back of a farm woman and hung on to her kerchief. Our cook, Darya, drunk as usual, dropped the eggs from under the geese, so that only three hatched out. Our pig has a nasty habit of biting people and eating our Indian corn. We've bought a calf for six rubles and she keeps on serenading us in a low bass voice.

All he knows about agriculture, he says, is that the earth is black. His debt depresses him, but he forgets it as he puzzles over the proper way to sow wheat and clover. The snow gives way to the mud of the thaw, the starlings return, the nightingales sing, the frogs are croaking. Soon his brothers and their families and a predatory crowd of visitors arrive, and just as he had had to do in Moscow, he is eventually obliged to leave the house and write in a one-room chalet he has rigged up. Among the visitors is a friend of his sister's from Moscow, Lika Mizinova, to whom he writes teasing notes.

Ah, lovely Lika! when you bedewed my right shoulder with your tears (I have taken out the spots with benzine), and when slice after slice you ate our bread and meat, we greedily devoured your face and head with our eyes. . . . Ah, Lika, Lika, diabolical beauty! . . . When you are at the Alhambra with Trofimov [an imaginary lover], I hope you may accidentally jab out his eye with your fork.

Other visitors are Lydia Yavorskaya, a young actress whom he called a "hussy," and a sentimental young novelist, Lydia

Avilova, whose manuscript he had read. He gave her sound
and very Chekhovian advice on writing:

> When you want to touch the reader's heart, try to be
> colder. It gives their grief as it were, a background,
> against which it stands out in greater relief. As it is,
> your heroes weep and you sigh.

At Melikhovo he was soon appointed "cholera superinten-
dent doctor" (for twenty-five villages, which included four
factories and one monastery)—also "sanitary attendant" for
the zemstvo (district council) without remuneration. He
drives about in a scurvy carriage. He has begged lime, vitriol
and "all sorts of stinking stuff" from the manufacturers,
necessary when cholera comes nearer.

It was important to him that this work was a matter of
private conscience. When cholera creeps as near as twenty
miles from the place, he goes begging for money from his
rich neighbors. On one of his begging missions he goes to
a rich landowner's house where he is treated *de haut en bas*
as a tiresome official, and he puts the rich man and his wife
at a loss by pretending to be a millionaire. He had little
respect for the country gentry, who had no sense of public
obligation and who, as we see in *The Wife*, passed their days
and nights in gluttonous eating, heavy drinking and playing
cards, patronizing everyone, especially doctors, as being beyond the pale. They dismissed the peasants as cadgers and
thieves.

Chekhov complains that his doctoring in this period has
stopped him from writing. What he meant was that he was

not finishing what he wrote. In his letters he says that he is kept going financially by the royalties from a one-act "vaudeville," *The Bear*, which he had scribbled out years before. Now he turns to an unfinished story, one in which Sakhalin becomes Russia itself. The story, *Ward 6*, is one of the most intense, powerful and claustrophobic he ever wrote. He was eight months writing it and it runs to fifty pages. When Lenin read it in his youth he said it had made him a revolutionary: for ourselves it may seem to foretell Solzhenitsyn's *Cancer Ward*.

We are struck first by the plain austerity of Chekhov's style. The narrator investigates the dreadful condition of an out-of-date hospital (such as many Chekhov must have seen when he was organizing resistance to the cholera). The hospital stands in a barren wilderness outside the town: the only other building in sight is the prison. We see the patients in the crowded wards, hear of the corrupt sale of drugs and medicines. Then the outside narrator slips away and the scene moves into the close-up of a particular room, Ward 6, in which five lunatics are isolated. Dr. Ragin, in charge of the hospital, is visiting them. All except one of the lunatics belong to the artisan class. There is a laborer who simply stares at the floor all day; another is a post-office sorter who gazes secretively from time to time at a medal under his shirt. He believes he has been awarded the Stanislas Medal and that he will shortly get the Swedish medal of the Golden Star. Another is a harmless Jew who went mad when his hat factory was destroyed in a fire—the only patient who is allowed out into the town, where he begs for a ruble or two and is the butt of the shopkeepers. The fifth, Gromov, is an educated paranoiac who gradually went mad after his father was imprisoned for fraud. Gromov believes he is guilty of murder. They are supervised by a warder, a brutal ex-soldier, who beats the lunatics when they become restive.

Dr. Ragin strikes us at first as being a concerned and humane man. He is aware that the hospital is scandalously out-of-date and offers nothing from the great advances in medicine of the last thirty years. He is drawn to Gromov, who has a sharp intellect and is a good talker in a destructive way, even if he will, in the end, fly into a paranoiac rage. To Ragin he is the only man in the hospital with whom he can discuss serious subjects, or indeed in the self-satisfied little town outside. He has stopped going out into local "society." He consoles himself with serious philosophical reading, and he and Gromov have arguments about Marcus Aurelius and stoicism and dispute the necessity of suffering. Gromov *is* mad and Ragin is trying to calm him. Conversation is the spell. At one point he makes the distinctly Chekhovian remark that "books are the printed score, while talk is the singing." Gromov will attack Ragin's arguments savagely one day and the next he will be languid. Ragin likes Gromov's voice, his young intelligent face, and he even admires the man's anger when he admits his mania and cries out that there are moments when he is overwhelmed by the thirst for life and begs for news of the outside world. Ragin makes regular visits to the Ward. Gromov suddenly asks him what will turn out to be a disturbing question:

"Have you any idea of suffering? Allow me to ask you, were you ever thrashed in your childhood?"

(This is, of course, one of Chekhov's own obsessive memories.) Ragin says he was not. Gromov pounces:

> "No one has laid a finger on you all your life. . . . You grew up under your father's wing and studied at his expense, and then you dropped at once into a sinecure. For more than twenty years you have lived rent-free with heating, lighting and service all provided. . . . You have handed over your work to the assistant and the rest of the rabble while you sit in peace and warmth, save money, read, amuse yourself with reflections, with all sorts of lofty nonsense, and [looking at Ragin's florid peasant face] with boozing."

Yes, in his self-isolated life in the hospital, Ragin has become a tippling conformist, his mind closed to change. Hospital regulations are a cocoon or simply a convenient private study.

The drama now is reversed. An ambitious young doctor, Khobotov, is intriguing to climb into Ragin's job. The rumor is spread that Ragin's visits to Ward 6 are suspect, a sign of "tiredness," "illness," or perhaps worse. He is summoned before a small informal commission of local doctors and officials (essentially a trial of his sanity), after which it is suggested that he should go on holiday. He gladly does so with the only friend he has in the town, an amiable, irresponsible postmaster, who takes him on a trip to Petersburg, Moscow and Warsaw. The postmaster is an average lazy, unreliable "good fellow," a genial liar, who is eager for a spree and thinks the trip will do Ragin good. This is the necessary "moment of rest" in the story, the point at which it will turn. Halfway through the holiday Ragin is bored by "the real world of pleasure." His will goes. While the postmaster goes out looking for women, gambling, losing his money and borrowing heavily from Ragin—money he will never repay—Ragin lies all day in the hotel, his face turned to the wall. "Real happiness," he says, "is impossible without solitude." When he returns to the hospital he finds that Khobotov has taken his job. Ragin utters an alarming phrase: "I have got into an enchanted circle." Indeed he has: Khobotov slyly puts Ragin into Ward 6 and Gromov is triumphant.

> "So they have put you in here too. You sucked the blood of others, and now they will suck yours."

And, sarcastically,

> "You should be philosophical."

When Ragin goes to the door to leave the ward, and complains, the warder knocks him out. Mad or not, Ragin dies of a stroke. Chekhov took pride in evoking this death in detail and is as effective in the last visions of the dying as he was in the death scene in *Gusev:*

> [Gromov] and millions of people believed in immortality. . . . But [Ragin] did not want immortality, and he thought of it only for one instant. A herd of deer, extraordinarily beautiful and graceful, of which he had

been reading the day before, ran by him; then a peasant woman stretched out her hand to him with a registered letter.

That registered letter! How perfect that random, final item of his vision is.

In his letters Chekhov was surprisingly offhand or defensive about *Ward 6*. This is partly due to his modesty or perhaps also to his awareness that to create characters whose opinions are simplifications of a conflict in his own nature was no more than analysis and derived from his reading. The contrast between the man who believes in a gospel of endurance derived from Marcus Aurelius (whose *Meditations* were very influential reading all over Europe at that time) and the man who rebels against his chains is a matter of fruitless debate. To judge from Chekhov's reply to a letter from Suvorin—who seems to have suggested the story was "lemonade" and needed more "alcohol"—Chekhov was almost submissive when he replied that this was an illness of his generation. In short, for Suvorin the story was a passive allegory when it ought to have had the dramatic force of parable. The great masters of the past not merely were good writers, but, Chekhov said, make one feel that

they are going towards something . . . have some object, just like the ghost of Hamlet's father, who did not come and disturb the imagination for nothing. . . . And we? . . . We paint life as it is, but beyond that—nothing at all.

He also agreed that the story stinks of the hospital and the mortuary.

And he writes, perhaps slyly, to the incurably sentimental and pursuing Lydia Avilova:

> I am finishing a story ("Ward No. 6"), a very dull one, owing to a complete absence of woman and the element of love. I can't endure such stories.

The truth remains that if Chekhov has projected a frightening and sterile universe, the line-by-line events of the story are powerful and blasting. Perhaps he felt that the irony of a situation in which a prison governor himself becomes voluntary prisoner was too neat. Ragin is a portrait of a governor who has come to think the real criminals are outside the walls. The truth is that the story is a study of the nightmare of absolute solitude.

One more story closes what has been called the "clinical" period of Chekhov's writing at Melikhovo, *The Black Monk*, and it is much weaker. It sprang, according to his sister, from a dream that had excited Chekhov one afternoon at Melikhovo. Here, Kovrin, the dreamer, is suffering from nervous exhaustion. He is staying on the enormous estate of a certain Pesotsky, who has barbered his trees into bizarre shapes, as if in mockery of Nature. Kovrin marries Tanya, the daughter of the house, and becomes a university professor, all the while feeling that he has betrayed his genius by keeping healthy and leading a normal life. This obsession is strengthened by hallucinations when he comes to imagine himself being visited by the Black Monk of the title. This visionary figure comes gliding over the grounds and tells Kovrin that he is ill because his genius puts him above the common herd and is incompatible with mortal love and that he will soon die. Kovrin is in a state of nervous breakdown, and on the monk's final visit he falls to the ground spitting blood: "his frail human body could no longer serve as the mortal garb of genius." He dies with "a blissful smile . . . upon his face."

An allegory of Chekhov's inner life at Melikhovo? A passing, visiting intuition of what Chekhov knows about his own dilemma as a sick man, an artist and an evasive lover? Or, at the lowest, a neat fantasy the writer is turning to account? There are poetical moments—particularly when the monk comes softly as a shadow passing over the miles of fields, taking away the light from the grasses and trees— that are as evocative as the strange sight of the deer that passes before the eyes of Dr. Ragin in *Ward 6*. But until that moment, the narrative in *The Black Monk* is far too mannered and bookish. Chekhov himself spoke of it as a study of megalomania, but he has forgotten his own rule: the essential thing, when one is writing about strong or strange feelings, is to be ice-cold.

We may be guessing, for good stories do not come straight from real experience but evolve from contemplating an essence of it, but this story could very well spring from a precise instance of self-isolation in Chekhov's life. We remember that his sister's friend Lika Mizinova often stayed at Melikhovo. She was fascinated by his talk. Did he see that the girl was in love with him? Did he fall back on his usual fantastic jokes in self-defense? Again, he pretends she is captivated by "the Circassian Levitan" and that he has just had a charming letter from the artist containing expressions like "The devil flay you: the devil choke you." To Levitan he has supposedly answered:

> If you don't stop pursuing Lika I'll shove a corkscrew into you, cheap riff-raff. Don't you know that Lika belongs to me and that we already have two children.

Lika would write back with annoyance, accusing him of egoism. Eventually she wrote him plainly in 1893:

> You know quite well how I feel about you and I am not ashamed to write about it. I know also that your behaviour to me is condescending and indifferent.

In the summer of 1893 Potapenko, a young journalist from Odessa, came to stay at Melikhovo. He was a good singer and Lika accompanied him on the piano. She had notions of becoming an actress or opera singer and she may have turned to him in order to make Chekhov jealous. She went back to Moscow and wrote to him:

> I must know whether you are coming to Moscow, and when, or not at all. It is all the same but I have to know. Only two months remain to me in which to see you, after that perhaps never.

Chekhov wrote to her:

Lika, when will it be spring? Accept [this] question literally and do not seek for a hidden meaning in it. Alas, I am already an old young man, my love is no sun and does not make a spring for me. . . . It is not you whom I so ardently love. I love in you my sufferings of the past and my now perished youth.

And again he wrote to her:

You say I used to be younger. Yes, imagine! I have passed thirty some time ago and already feel forty close at hand. I have grown old, not in body only, but in spirit. . . . I get up and go to bed feeling as though interest in life had dried up in me.

These are not the words of a cold-hearted man who is amusing himself. He was indeed self-protective: no saint but certainly not cruel. He had a strict conscience and yet one sees him restless, burning himself out. The gentle skeptical Chekhov is also the greedy observer. He will stand by his principles and yet be unknowable both in his reserve and in his laughter. In her old age and long after his death, his sister wrote about his feelings for Lika:

I do not know what was in my brother's mind, but that it seemed to me that he strove to overcome his feelings [for Lika]. In her there were certain traits alien to him: a lack of character and a fondness for a Bohemian existence.

Defeated, Lika had an affair in Paris with Potapenko. She soon found herself deserted, pregnant, wretched and alone in Switzerland. She wrote to Chekhov and told him her story. He replied:

> [T]hough you . . . taunt me with having rejected you, yet thank you all the same; I know perfectly well you are not going to die, and that no one has rejected you.

He himself went off on one of his sudden journeys to the south for his health. He says he simply must "write, write and write." And then comes the usual fantasy:

> Dear Lika, when you become a great singer and are paid a handsome salary, then be charitable to me, marry me, keep me at your expense, that I may be free to do nothing.

There is something odd about Chekhov's journey. There were indeed two journeys: one with Potapenko in August 1894 down the Volga, in which Potapenko said nothing about his betrayal of Lika, and another, three weeks later, when Chekhov went off again to see his uncle Mitrofan, who was dying, then on an erratic trip to Odessa, Lvov, Vienna, Abbazia, Trieste and Venice, where he caught nettle rash, on to Genoa, whose ornate cemetery he visited, and finally to Nice, where he found the letter from Lika that told her wretched story. She was in Switzerland:

There is not a trace of the old Lika left and I cannot really say that you are to blame for it. . . . If you are not afraid to be disappointed you may come. . . . Still I don't think you will cast a stone at me. It seems to me you were always indifferent.

Later she wrote: "What was I to do, Daddy?"

He replied that he was *not* indifferent to people, and that is indeed true, but he did not visit her in Switzerland. It is odd that he went on these long haphazard journeys; odder too that before he left he did not tell his family and even forgot to leave them with money.

Chekhov had supposed that Abbazia would be an innocent, antiquated little place. It turned out to be a new tourist trap, with up-to-date hotels where the rich Russian landowners, with their wives or mistresses, confided their debts or their love affairs at the top of their voices, very much in the manner of Ivanov in his play of that name. Chekhov uses Abbazia as the background to a short scene in his story *Ariadne*, which also has some Italian background. Ariadne is a beautiful, fickle young woman. She contracts a liaison with a landowner, Shamokhin, and the story consists of his frustrations and sufferings, as confided in the narrator, an author by profession. Shamokhin says that when Germans or English meet they talk of nothing but their business or their crops, whereas

[we Russians] discuss nothing but abstract subjects and women. . . . A mediocre philosopher like Max Nordau would explain these incessant conversations about women as a form of erotic madness, or would put it down to our having been slave-owners. . . . I take . . . a different view. . . . we are dissatisfied [with women] because we are idealists.

He evokes Ariadne's spell when he knew her as a willful and spoiled young girl who so fascinated him that he has almost ruined himself and his father to pay for her extravagances. He believes he can hold her by educating her, for he sees her predatory habits arise from lack of education, and he has been dragging her around art galleries and museums and has introduced her to celebrated and learned men. She simply pretends to know what they are talking about; indeed she is a natural liar in everything. This comedy is well done, for Ariadne is not a caricature of the socialite, though it must be said that Chekhov does rather press his serious view that women need to be emancipated and trained, as males are trained. To be brought up only as a sheltered wife and mother is wrong. Considering the idleness of Shamokhin, his talk is comic. On the other hand, there is no doubt of Ariadne's beauty and allure. She loves her beautiful body and its spell and is entranced by gazing at it. She is proud of her erotic nature. (Earlier, in *The Duel*, Chekhov had shown some Tolstoyan disgust when, in his account of the bedroom scene, the lady herself has no shame.)

In Petersburg the gossip was that *Ariadne* was drawn from the actress Yavorskaya, who was briefly Chekhov's mistress and who was notorious for her passion for publicity. She had once stayed at Melikhovo because Chekhov was "a famous man" and the acquaintance would give a push to her career. She said that Chekhov had been in love with her. She encouraged the rumor and was far from displeased by the tale. She later intrigued for a part in *The Seagull* but there he firmly turned her down.

In *An Anonymous Story* Chekhov turns a possible Ariadne into a very different figure. It is an unbelievable venture into the glossy well-worn subject of the Sins of Society. Perhaps it springs from his observation of the rich and cynical company Suvorin kept in Petersburg, a city Chekhov hated. *An Anonymous Story* is a confession. We see a young naval officer who has joined a secret group of terrorists disguise himself as a footman to a rich top Petersburg official called Orlov in order to spy on him and go through his papers. The weakness of the story is that we never see or hear of any of the "footman's" comrades or their "Cause." Dostoyevsky had never made that kind of mistake. Orlov has a mistress, a married woman (Zinaida), who insists on leaving home and coming to live with him, much to his dismay. The "footman" falls in love with her, studies her, obeys her orders and notes her determination to take charge of Orlov's household. She even wants to cook, and yet she has been reading Turgenev and sees herself, he thinks, as the luxurious Odintsova in *Fathers and Sons*. When the corrupt Orlov is unfaithful to her the "footman" nobly rescues her and escapes with her to Nice and Venice. The two are not lovers, for she is pregnant by Orlov and indeed dies in giving birth to a baby girl. There is even a suggestion that she has poisoned herself. The plot and scene are plain Ouida: it is an odd fact that Chekhov had read Ouida with admiration! Before the girl's death the "footman" confesses that he has broken with the terrorists on principle. She comes to life in our minds when she points out that he has done this simply because he has no character, no will of his own. She knows his only "terrorist" act had been slapping the face of one of Orlov's important friends with a bunch of newspapers! The good things in the story are the thumbnail portraits of Orlov's corrupt, card-playing and wenching friends. There is also a neat portrait of Zinaida's thieving maid. Orlov's polished cynicism is well observed. Chekhov noted that Orlov reads a great deal but that "even when he reads" there is a look of irony on his face. Chekhov admitted that he had "botched" the end of the tale.

It is a relief to see him turning to the world he really knows in two genuine stories: *The Teacher of Literature*, into which he dipped when he came to writing *The Three Sisters*; and the one he once called his favorite among all his works, *The Student*. It is certainly one of his most tender, subtle and poetic allegories. It may have been suggested by the simple religious parables that Tolstoy was writing at this time, or by the pious Leskov's mystical tales, though, unlike Leskov, Chekhov was a confirmed atheist. Chekhov's story takes a step far beyond trite religious insinuation, and if it is a parable, it is a parable about the imagination. On the eve of Good Friday a young and pious theological student is seen walking home along empty marshland in a bitterly cold wind and he is thinking:

[J]ust such a wind had blown in the days of Ryurik and in the time of Ivan the Terrible and Peter [the Great], and . . . there had been just the same desperate poverty and hunger, the same thatched roofs with holes in them, ignorance, misery, the same desolation around, the same darkness, the same feeling of oppression—all these had existed, did exist, and would exist, and the lapse of a thousand years would make life no better.

He comes upon two widowed peasant women, a mother and her daughter, who live in an almshouse. They are sitting by a bonfire in the garden, washing up their bowls and spoons, and he joins them to warm his frozen hands by their fire. They tell him they have been to a Bible meeting— professional news for a naïve young theologian. He holds out his hands to the fire and to profit by the occasion he says, "At just such a fire the Apostle Peter warmed himself . . . so it must have been cold then, too." And then he is impelled to remind them, almost as gossip, of how, little by little, Saint Peter had denied Christ three times before the Crucifixion. And as he goes on, earnestly bringing to life that faraway time, he notices that the older woman is moved to sob "as though ashamed of her tears," and that the young woman, who had in her time been beaten to a state of stupidity by her husband, has become tense like "someone enduring intense pain." The student leaves them, pleased at first by his skill in bringing to present life an old story, and then he begins to wonder why the woman wept.

[It was] not because he could tell the story touchingly . . . but because her whole being was interested in what was passing in Peter's soul. And joy suddenly stirred in his soul, and he even stopped for a minute to take breath. The past, he thought, is linked with the present by an unbroken chain of events flowing one out of another . . . when he touched one end the other quivered . . . that truth and beauty which had guided human life there in the garden and in the yard of the high priest had continued without interruption to this day and had evidently always been the chief thing in human life and in all earthly life, indeed; and the feeling of youth, health, vigour—he was only twenty-two—and the inexpressible sweet expectation of happiness, took possession of him little by little, and life seemed to him enchanting, marvelous and full of lofty meaning.

Chapter Eleven

The summers at Melikhovo were delectable, but the winters were severe. By 1893, when he was thirty-three, Chekhov was still slaving half the week at the book on Sakhalin, which was being serialized in the "thick journal" *Russian Thought*, and the rest of the week working on the stories. There were exhausting trips to Moscow and Petersburg, where he restlessly "feasted," as he said, with his friends. There was a price: he returned with what he called bronchitis caused, he said, by smoking cigars. He gave them up. He groaned about his debts and added to the work in hand his official duties as sanitary inspector of the hospitals of his region and on the zemstvo, the local council. He had become deeply depressed and talked wildly of going abroad—to South Africa, Japan and India—more precisely, of joining Tolstoy's son Leo on a trip to the World's Fair in Chicago! Nothing came of these dreams of travel. One reason for his depression, his brother Alexander said after a querulous visit to Melikhovo, was that he was shut up in the tedious company of his father and his simple mother, with whom he had nothing in common. Alexander said, "What sense is there in letting the

A la Tremontanas devour your soul the way the rats devour candles." (This absurd word was the nickname the sons had given their father.) Alexander begged his brother to give up the dream of idyllic peace of country life. Anton listened and said nothing. He had become notoriously an apparent listener who, even in more exciting company than Alexander's, was given to uttering apparently irrelevant yet gnomic or fantastic comments that killed the subject. He had once interrupted a wrangling discussion of Marxism with the eccentric suggestion: "Everyone should visit a stud farm. It is very interesting," as if his mind were wandering. Was the remark so irrelevant? Chekhov's apparent perversities were sly. The peace of country life? The industrial revolution had seeped in here and there into the country around Melikhovo. As a doctor Chekhov saw disturbing instances of a new sickness. The traditional idle landowners and the ignorant peasants were being replaced by a new race: the factory owners, enterprising and ruthless men from the towns.

Chekhov's concern at first is with the lives of the wives and daughters of the rich manufacturers whose homes are attached to the factory sites. His impressions are those of a doctor and are diagnoses. In *A Doctor's Visit* we hear the hellish noises of the factory and are told of the boring, squalid lives of the workers. The industrial dust lies on the leaves of the lilac trees near the factory. Chekhov is a man for sounds. We hear the metallic banging made by the watchmen to warn off intruders, we sense the military nature of the organization. We see the third-rate oil paintings and terrible chandeliers of the factory owner's house. The husband has died, but his widow lives fretfully on, tarnished by a dreary life; her daughter is on the point of a nervous breakdown. She is isolated in the home, emotionally starved, and is ruled by the classic greedy governess who is "in heaven" because *she* can now eat food and drink wine that were beyond her means before she took the job.

In the long story *A Woman's Kingdom* there is a variation of the factory theme. Here a woman has inherited an iron works from her uncle. Although her father was his brother's heir, he was kept "in the position of a workman [and] paid . . . sixteen rubles a month," so the woman had grown up as the daughter of a "simple workman." She hates the falsity of her new position and bitterly regrets leaving her class. Chekhov admired the novels of Zola, though, unlike Zola, he is never melodramatic. Chekhov is the doctor examining the moral sickness of industrial life, and his style remains quietly concerned and expository. He is never lush or theatrical.

He now turns to the commercial aspect of industrialism in *Three Years*, the chronicle of the Laptev family, whose founder has come up to Moscow from the provinces and becomes a millionaire. He makes his money in wholesale haberdashery, buying cheap, selling dear and keeping the wages of his large staff down. The father is a miserable fellow, sentimental and pious in family life, but an "Asiatic despot" in his huge warehouse. The firm is probably drawn from the one in which Chekhov's father had been humbly employed after his flight as a bankrupt from Taganrog. The staff are obliged to "live in"; they take all their meals in the canteen; they are marched en masse to church on Sundays and old Laptev shrewdly controls them by trading on their anxieties.

> Bonuses were given to all the clerks every year, but privately, so that the man who got little was bound from vanity to say he had got more. . . . Nothing was strictly forbidden, and so the clerks never knew what was allowed, and what was not.

Old Laptev has two sons, who are crippled by their wealth. The younger plays the fool in self-defense and goes mad; the elder makes a loveless marriage with a genteel and pious provincial girl who has married him for his money and middle-class security. The marriage is disappointing at first, but she grows fonder of her husband as the story progresses. Before his marriage he had vague "artistic" interests. He had had a mistress but now dreads the "inconvenience" of meeting her in Moscow, although he hankers after her. The mistress is said to have been drawn from the noisy Kundasova, the independent Bohemian friend of Suvorin and Chekhov, whom they called the "astronomer." (She had worked in an observatory.) In the story she turns up in Moscow, cheerfully hard up, and she gets a living by giving piano lessons. She is on good terms with Yartsev, a Bohemian polyglot and writer who lives precariously by his wits.

Three Years has been called Chekhov's "Hymn to Moscow," and if that is so, it is Yartsev who shouts it out at the top of his voice. Unlike the colorless Laptev, he has imagination and is one of Chekhov's Gogolian eccentrics. In a cab ride through the beautiful Moscow parks Yartsev's fantasies run wild at the sight of the famous sunsets. Villages are on fire, he cries out, hordes of Asiatic savages are pouring in.

> One of them, a terrible old man with a bloodstained face all scorched from the fire, binds to his saddle a young girl with a white Russian face, and the girl looks sorrowful, understanding. . . . A huge wild boar, frantic with terror, rushed through the village. . . . And the girl tied to the saddle was still looking.

The chronicle rambles on in its year-to-year tour of middle-class gentility, sexual frustration, familial worry and second-rate tastes. There is a small scene, absurd yet sympathetic, when the older Laptev brother is seen going in for Art and taking his wife to buy a picture at an art exhibition. With an air she poses and looks at the pictures "as her husband did, through her open fist or an opera glass." She then drifts into a daydream and imagines herself walking through the countryside the artist has depicted. When she goes home she is angry about the vulgar pictures her husband has bought and all the knickknacks he has collected. At the end of the story we shall see her daring to wake up and venturing on flirtations with her husband's friends. One is reminded of the chronicles of petit bourgeois ups and downs, of puzzled shames and resignations, in English and French novels of the period.

If Chekhov's alacrity is dimmed by the duties of this long chronicle, it revives in *An Anna on the Neck*, written in the same year. This is set in the provinces. We see an eighteen-year-old girl forced to marry a pompous official of fifty-two because her father has ruined the family by heavy drinking. Anna is glad to get away from her sordid home and she will become as dominant and predatory as the grander lady in *Ariadne*; but what will remain in our minds is the guilt of the father as he says good-bye at the railway station when the honeymoon couple go off:

> Anna leaned out of the window towards him and he whispered something to her, enveloping her in stale wine-fumes, blowing into her ear—it was impossible to understand what he was saying—and making the sign of the cross over her face and breast and hands. . . . Anna's brothers, Petya and Andryusha, schoolboys, tugged at his coat from behind and whispered in embarrassment. "Papa, stop it . . . Don't Papa."
>
> When the train moved, Anna saw her father running a little way after it, staggering and splashing wine out of his glass, and saw how pathetic and kind and guilty he looked.
>
> "Hurrah!" he shouted.

That "Hurrah!" will haunt us with its absurdity and pathos; the crushed girl is entitled to her shameless and successful revenge. It will be at the unloved husband's expense.

Chapter Twelve

By the spring of 1895 Chekhov had been three years at Melikhovo and had contrived to make his responsibilities as a son, a concerned landowner, a doctor and restless writer interlock. As for money, it was always short. In Russia, he says, the smallest success in farming is gained only at the price of a cruel struggle with nature: "You have to take the axe and scythe yourself." Still, his copse has grown a yard taller and "will make capital for my heirs, who will call me an ass, for heirs are never satisfied." We reflect on his secret bad health: at the heart of that concern is his responsibility to his parents and his sister. But for her devotion to him his sister might well have married.

In this year, 1895, his writing was interrupted by a conference of doctors in the province. They inspected hospitals. Then Chekhov turned to building a new school; the old one was dark, poorly furnished and not fit for teachers or children. Chekhov, helped by his sister, drew up plans, dealt with the contractors about bricks, mortar and timber, and pressed for higher pay for the wretched schoolteachers. In January and February 1897 Chekhov helped to conduct the national census of that year. He had to traipse from one peasant hut to another, knocking his head on the low doorways, carrying "detestable inkpots," wearing an official badge, and carrying a portfolio into which the census forms did not fit.

When they turned from Chekhov's life at Melikhovo during this period to the story *The House with the Mezzanine*, his readers were at first astonished to see that he seemed to be attacking everything he believed in. How was it possible that the builder of schools, libraries, the advocate of better hospitals, the practical worker in popular education could ridicule a young educated woman who is giving her life to these practical and enlightened causes? She is no idle do-gooder who forgets to attack the root of the matter—the government official who is the source of the corruption of the province. When the story begins we see at once that Chekhov has been careful to unself himself by turning the narrative over to a narrator unlike himself: an idle landscape painter. To get away from his host, a local landowner, whose conversation is tedious, the painter wanders about the idyllic countryside and discovers a charming little house owned by a pleasant old lady and her two good-looking daughters. One is a public-spirited teacher, the other an idle girl of seventeen who sits about reading. Antagonism arises between him and the teacher. He is soon arguing that her attempts to enlighten the peasants are futile, that education, libraries, even medical centers are useless. The misery, the very ignorance of the peasants, arises from back-breaking physical labor. (The liberal editor of *Russian Thought*, Vukol Lavrov, had heard this argument from Chekhov himself.)

The elder sister is domineering. She is nevertheless excellent in argument as she fights back. What use is landscape painting? And she makes one deadly point: the painter's landscapes lack an indispensable element—they have no people in them. Her temper and no doubt her jealousy are aroused when she sees the painter and her sister falling in love. Drastically and secretly she packs the young girl away to stay with distant relations, the end of the affair that has not even had a farewell kiss.

If landscape with its indifference to people pervades the debate in *The House with the Mezzanine*, it has little place in the theme of fierce class conflict in *My Life*, one of Chekhov's longest and most vigorous stories. In its freedom from the episodic weakness of *Three Years* it has the elaborate and sustained design of a short novel. It clearly derives from Chekhov's experience in building schools and working with the common run of manual laborers: the carpenters, roofers and painters, and also with the peasants, whom he has now intimately observed. Again, he had been reading Zola's studies of class conflict, and although he rejected Zola's forced afflatus and his spells of orgiastic sexual symbolism, he admired his careful social realism. What gives *My Life* its special force is that his own imagination has been refreshed once more by a return to the scenes of his boyhood in Taganrog. His early conflict with his father, old Pavel, has been brought forward and reconsidered in the light of ideas closer to experience in our own century. The father, who had been a bankrupt shopkeeper, now reappears as a provincial architect, still believing that he is filled "with the divine fire," who builds ugly and pretentious houses. The real Pavel—whom we had seen in the story *Difficult People* and who ruled by beating his sons—is now succeeded by a fictional father who strikes his son in the face and hits him with his umbrella. But the father is more than half romantic in his pretensions: he has given his son and daughter affected names, Misail and Cleopatra, suited to grown children who have been brought up to marry into the genteel families of the town.

It is his son, Misail, who writes the story of his revolt, and in the first person. The revolt is not simply a conflict with his father: it is a revolt against the corrupt money-making respectability and ethos of the ruling citizens of the town itself. Misail is not a political figure. As many critics have noticed, he is an early example of our contemporary "dropout." We see him refusing to "get ahead" in the necessary office job. He has in fact lost nine office jobs, and not only his father but the whole town turns against him as he drifts into earning a precarious living as an ill-paid laborer in the building trade, without a decent home. The sight of him in mud- and paint-stained workman's clothes in the streets of the town arouses jeers, and shopkeepers enjoy throwing a pail of dirty water over him from their doorways as he passes. At one time, when he is out of work, a friendly butcher, Prokofy, hires him to work in the slaughterhouse and this leads to an absurd scene with the governor of the province, who summons him to explain his rebellion. The governor remonstrates with him, suggesting that he should change his way of life or leave the area. When Misail goes to his interview wearing his stinking bloodstained clothes, the governor asks him if he is a vegetarian! A Chekhovian joke? Yes—but double-edged. Vegetarians pass as shiftless and disaffected religious sectarians in the town, to the point of being politically dangerous, or even "holy fools." Misail's rebellion gives him an intimate knowledge of the realities of working-class life and especially of the painters and roof builders. At first they too regard him as a crank and a fool, but then accept him because he works hard, though they are somewhat put out when he will not join them in stealing paint and cadging drinks from employers. Misail becomes particularly friendly with one craftsman, nicknamed Radish, a venturesome and crankish roofer:

He walked the roofs as freely as though he were on the ground. In spite of his being ill and pale as a corpse, his agility was extraordinary: he used to paint the domes and cupolas of the church, without scaffolding, like a young man, with only the help of a ladder and a rope, and it was rather horrible when, standing at a height far from the earth, he would draw himself erect and for some unknown reason pronounce: "Lice consume grass, rust consumes iron and lying the soul." Or, thinking about something, would speak his thoughts aloud: "Anything may happen. Anything may happen."

Presently the story and its scene widens. Enter the engineer who is in charge of building a new railway, a shrewd fellow, also of working-class origin, who once had a job as a greaser in Belgium. He has learned to like luxury and has bought up the houses of the ruined landowners and has given his pretty daughter an excellent education. (We have seen such a character as the engineer in Chekhov's early story *Lights*.) He is blunt to Misail, who belongs to the gentry class by origin, and he sees his daughter is in love with him. Like any self-made man, he is sentimental. He encourages their idyll. They marry and he gives them one of his large country houses. His daughter longs to farm "by the book." Here, Misail is up against another breed of manual laborers—the medieval Russian peasants. He sows and scythes but the peasants are wholesale thieves. They demand vodka by the keg, they make off with his crops openly by the wagonload, they brawl and tear up his garden. The young wife is terrified of them, and on one frightful night Misail has to rush outside to grapple with two men who are fighting. This episode confirms his wife's growing dislike of rural life and contributes to the decision which she takes to leave him. He understands this decision and has to let her go. She wants to join her father, who has gone to America to build a railway, and Misail goes back to his life as a painter and builder.

Misail has only two friends besides Radish. One is a young and plausible doctor who argues that Misail's proper duty to society lies in being a thinker, a scientist and intellectual, advancing civilization and the cause of human freedom. Misail's other friend is his unmarried sister, who covertly slips away from their father when she can, to console her brother. The young doctor often joins them. Why? It is one of the great merits of the story that Misail is slow to know what is going on in his sister's mind. In her longing to get away from home she is in love with the doctor, is entranced by his talk of freedom—also, naïvely, by his dressy appearance. He is a military doctor and has a wife and three children in

Petersburg. Misail doesn't guess that his sister has been seduced by the doctor and his talk of freedom in love, and is pregnant. The scene of revelation is masterly. She is asked to take part in an amateur theatrical organized by a ludicrous couple who regard themselves as the leading patrons of the arts in the town. She goes, but on the little stage she forgets her lines, drops down to her knees, and bursts out sobbing. The hostess cries out, "She is with child," and insists that Misail take her away at once. At the end of the story we learn that the sister has died in childbirth. The child is a little girl.

There is nothing sentimental or melodramatic in *My Life*. Misail tells his story honestly and plainly. Dryly, he says he is now respected in the town for his austerity. He is indifferent to pity. Like Chekhov, he is a stoic. He is now a contractor, trusted in his job, and admits he bores his workers by his moralizings. As a chronicler, he is still recording the daily stupidities of the town. Again, like Chekhov himself, he is an ardent reader of the press: "When we had the cholera [he writes], Prokofy cured the shopkeepers with pepper-brandy and tar and took money for it, and as I read in the newspaper, he was flogged for libeling the doctors as he sat in his shop." Misail takes his sister's little girl to see her mother's grave. He is not withdrawn; he observes that the shopkeepers no longer throw pails of water on him as he passes down the street, though he does note that he is older, stern, rarely laughing, and has been told that he has become like "Radish."

Chapter Thirteen

In August 1895 Chekhov visited Tolstoy and stayed a day and a half with him. Tolstoy's play *The Power of Darkness* had had a success at Suvorin's little theater. Tolstoy made a "marvelous impression" on Chekhov, and so did his daughters.

> They adore their father [Chekhov wrote Suvorin] and have a fanatical faith in him and that means that Tolstoy is a great moral force. . . . A man can deceive his fiancée or his mistress as much as he likes, and, in the eyes of a woman he loves, an ass may pass for a philosopher.

But "daughters are like sparrows: you don't catch them with empty chaff."

Then out came the news:

> Can you imagine it—I am writing a play which I shall probably not finish before the end of November. I am writing it not without pleasure, though I swear fearfully

at the conventions of the stage. It's a comedy, there are three women's parts, six men's, four acts, landscapes (view over a lake); a great deal of conversation about literature, little action, tons of love.

In a later letter to Suvorin he says of the play: "I began it *forte* and ended it *pianissimo*—contrary to all the rules of dramatic art. . . . [it] will be altered a million times before the coming season."

On top of that there is the censor. The privileged Tolstoy had absolutely refused to alter a line of *The Power of Darkness*. It was played exactly as he wrote it. Not so with Chekhov.

The play is *The Seagull*. As is well known, the first performance in Petersburg was a disaster, chiefly because Chekhov had allowed a popular music-hall actress—who had no part in the play—to use the occasion for her benefit night, and so a large part of the audience was drawn from fans of her romping farces. From the moment of Nina's exalted speech about the World Spirit, beginning

Men, lions, eagles, partridges, horned deer, . . . silent fishes, denizens of the deep, starfish and creatures invisible—in a word all life, all life has completed its cycle and died. For thousands of centuries Earth has not borne a single living creature. . . . Eternal Matter has turned them to stones, water, clouds . . .

and on to the claim

That World Spirit am I. . . . Within me is the soul of Alexander the Great, of Caesar, Shakespeare and Napoleon and of the most miserable leech . . .

Chekhov was satirizing a current fad. The audience shouted out "Intellectual rot" and were soon in a state of riot. When the dead seagull was brought in, a wit sitting next to a friend of Chekhov's shouted out, "Why does this Apollonsky [the actor who played Treplev] carry a dead duck about with him?" Hiding alone in a dressing room, Chekhov was appalled at what seemed to him an attack on his person, and left the theater. He said, "Not if I live to be seven hundred will I write another play."

When we look at the intimate sources of the play, we see that there was private embarrassment among Chekhov's closest friends. Chekhov's sister arranged for Lika Mizinova to go with her on the second night. Potapenko, who had made Lika pregnant but done nothing to help when their child was born, brought his wife with him. There were fears of "confrontations." There was also the question of the suicidal Levitan, the painter, who had earlier threatened a libel action when he had been portrayed years before in Chekhov's story *The Grasshopper*, but had recanted. Chekhov had once been called urgently, to a country house, near a lake, to save Levitan's life. He had attempted to shoot himself in the presence of a lady who had turned down his advances. And there was another real-life incident, which had occurred when he and Chekhov had gone out to shoot woodcock. Levitan had wounded a bird and was too distressed to kill it and had made Chekhov do the nasty job. There was no trouble with Levitan or with Potapenko after the play but Lika Mizinova did make one disturbing straightforward comment: "Everyone says *The Seagull* was borrowed from my life but also that you gave a good dressing down to a certain person." Who was that? Mizinova's defaulting lover Potapenko, obviously. But he was not the only one of Chekhov's friends to be pilloried, however obliquely, in *The Seagull*. The other was Lydia Avilova, who was still pursuing him, and to whom he sent a disguised teasing message in the text of the play.

What is certain is that *The Seagull* stands alone among Chekhov's plays, a marvelous lyrical experiment never repeated. It is spontaneously personal and quite unlike any of the plays he had written before. His earlier play, *Ivanov*, was dominated by a declamatory hero, the confession of the private guilt of a ruined landowner. Except for Nina's family the people of *The Seagull* are not traditional landowners. They are Bohemian artists, deep in literary confessions and theatrical illusions. The detached observer of their follies is a doctor. At the center of the play is the conflict of the young artists—the playwright Treplev and his sweetheart, Nina—with Treplev's mother, the famous and parsimonious old-style actress Arkadina, who talks only of her successful career. The deeper conflict is Oedipal. Chekhov borrows from *Hamlet*: Treplev is a young Hamlet, his mother is an absurd Gertrude seen in Shakespeare's dire "play within a play." The sexual jealousy is powerful and not concealed. The famous words "enseamed bed" are said to have been there; the censor was so shocked he cut them out.

The slave to literature is Trigorin, Arkadina's lover. He

draws Nina to him by telling her that his fame and glory as a novelist are empty; its fine effects are produced by cynical slavery to sentences. A writer who is enslaved by a famous actress, he says, is a prisoner.

Is Trigorin Chekhov's self-portrait? A good deal comes from Potapenko, the facile and popular best seller. Treplev, who hates Trigorin and dismisses him as a popular fiction machine, even picks out one of Chekhov's well-known sentences, in which he wrote that a gleam of moonlight is best evoked by pointing to the gleam reflected on a broken bottle. Trigorin's main resemblance to Chekhov lies in the keeping of notebooks in which he writes down subjects and people for stories, their mannerisms and absurdities, listing images and phrases that will be useful. He frankly tells Nina that words of hers will be useful in the novel he is writing. He has, he says, no personal life. There is the moment when, happening to see a cloud pass by, he suddenly sees it comically as "a grand piano" and writes the sentence at once in case it will at some time become useful. Chekhov's *Selected Notebooks* are indeed filled with bizarre sentences he has heard and characters he has met. At one point Trigorin is most certainly Chekhov when, talking of the hollowness of fame, he says that when he dies people will say, "A good writer, but not as good as Turgenev." Still, there is in Trigorin a good deal of Potapenko, who had gone off with Lika Mizinova and who annoyed Chekhov by the machinelike speed of his writing: a real best seller, and a seducer of women.

The interest of *The Seagull* lies in its break with traditional theater. The play is at once lyrical and bizarre: it mocks conventions. Chekhov has been excited by the new European playwrights—Ibsen (though he thought Ibsen novelized far too much), Hauptmann, Maeterlinck and above all, it strikes one, by the Strindberg of *Miss Julie*. Strindberg's short stories had loosened the restraints of formal speech and had released the spontaneous, even the incongruous, common utterance. The classic chorus had replaced the formal rhetoric of the ruling gods. That drilled moaning is now stopped; the crowds speak up variously; *they* are the gods now. They have replaced rhetoric by the utterance of their own histories and fantasies, each man and woman a walking inconsequent, self-portrayed creature carrying his own play about with him.

Why does the exalted young Treplev shoot himself at the end of the play? He has lost the love of Nina, the dream of success. His suicide is a revenge on his mother and her lover. His inner drama is too much for him. His vision of what theater ought to be, his desire to "go to the top" instantly, cannot be fulfilled because he lacks Nina's stamina, her willingness to go through the mill as an actress. There is something else: *The Seagull* is "strange" in its mingling of the artifices and isolating demands of art, the conflict with reality—that is to say, between two hostile realities. It is an alluring mixture of the poetic and the dire, an extravagant and disturbing dream.

At Melikhovo Chekhov tried to rid himself of his anger at the reception of *The Seagull* by turning to a new subject. His exhausting labor on the census had given him a theme of which he had long experience: the Russian peasant. We have already had a sight of the violence of peasant life in

My Life, which was at last published after a struggle with the censor; surprisingly, the public and the critics had little or nothing to say about it. Now, in *The Peasants*, villagers themselves fill the pages. This story made a powerful impression on its readers; it aroused a political storm, especially among Marxists and Populists, because Chekhov seemed hostile to the peasantry, which he was not; the Marxists welcomed his unvarnished picture but the Populists protested against it. There is no doubt that *The Peasants* is one of Chekhov's masterpieces and, on the same theme, will be surpassed only by *In the Ravine*, written a year or two later.

The Peasants has one of Chekhov's most casual beginnings and like so many of his finest stories is the tale of a journey, of departure and return, by which the leading characters are changed. A poor Moscow waiter in a luxury restaurant is dismissed from his job because of an accident. He has dropped a plate of ham and peas as he rushes it to a customer. Ill and desperate, he takes his wife, Olga, and his daughter, Sasha, to stay with their relations, who live in a filthy hut infested by flies in an isolated village. When they arrive all their relatives are out at work in the fields except for an unwashed and pathetic little girl who stands by the stove. Near her is a white cat.

"Puss, puss," Sasha called to her cat. "Puss!"

"She can't hear," said the little girl. "She has gone deaf."

"How is that?"

"She was beaten."

The visitors wait in the street until the family comes back from work. When they come, the story gradually develops into a year's chronicle of their lives as seen mainly through the eyes of the waiter's wife, Olga, a naïve peasant woman whose strength lies in the humble religious intimations we have already read of in *The Student*. Her religion may be literal and trite, but she knows the spell of archaic biblical words and has trained her daughter to use them and to be an echo of herself. In the course of a dreadful and riotous year she will awe her savage and quarreling relations. We shall see the quarrels, the young hurting the old, the ragged children huddled on the stove with their savage grandmother. We shall see a wife beaten, a young woman stripped naked. The village will catch fire and the men, drunk on vodka, scream for water; the children hope their neighbors will be burned to death; the geese, as savage as the people, seize the opportunity to raid the gardens; doves turn red as they fly over the flames of the burning huts; the tax collector comes round to collect arrears and goes off with the sacred samovars, the only treasure peasant women have. When the disaster is over we shall have a glimpse of the gentry and their sons and daughters in church on Sunday, and the waiter's daughter will copy her mother's singsong voice, saying,

"God lives in the church. Men have lamps and candles but God has little green and red and blue lamps, like little eyes. At night God walks about the church and with Him the Holy Mother of God and Saint Nicolai, thud, thud, thud. . . ."

When the end of the world comes the church itself will be carried to heaven. The myth silences the family crowded in the hut. Olga cries, not only because of the legend but also from pride in her daughter's telling of it.

We notice, throughout *The Peasants*, Chekhov's genius for seeing events as they strike his people differently, and above all his ear for the changing of sounds. When the village crops are on fire he gives us the confusion, but it is Olga who "makes it true" for us when we see her rushing out to save her daughter.

The terrible year of crowded events, in which the intruders are hated by their relatives, reaches a climax in the winter. The waiter dies after being cupped by the village tailor, a Jew who serves as a kind of doctor. In the spring, Olga and her daughter leave the village to go back on foot to Moscow. They are reduced to the condition of beggars. We see Olga and Sasha look back as they leave this hell, thinking how terrible the people were, worse than beasts, spending their lives stealing from each other, fighting. Yet, Olga reflects,

> they were human beings, they suffered and wept like human beings, and there was nothing in their lives for which one could not find excuse. . . . And now she felt sorry for all these people, painfully so, and as she walked on she kept looking back at the huts.

That "looking back," so casual, so impelled, is the perfect touch of nature. That is how we shall remember her. And Chekhov—a man who knows his art—will presently repeat the "looking back." Some miles further on Olga will pass another woman and, "looking back," will remember that she had met this woman in Moscow, perhaps as a cook to a rich family. The second "look back" brings home to Olga that she has no job and is herself now a beggar. Passing a grand house she sings out in a beggar's whine:

> "Good Christian folk, give alms, for Christ's sake, that God's blessing may be upon you, and that your parents may be in the Kingdom of Heaven in peace eternal."

And her daughter joins in, copying the voice of her mother, Again, agony is made real to us by hearing its echo.

The Peasants was a sensation when it was published. Chekhov's mastery was recognized by all the critics. The censor had cut out a page at the end. We notice that he will not stand for any hostile criticism of the police or tax collectors. The simple Olga reflects that if the peasants brutalize one another,

> they had none to whom they could look for help. . . . the paltriest little clerk or official treated the peasants as though they were tramps, and addressed even the village elders and church wardens as inferiors, and considered they had a right to do so. And, indeed, can any sort of help or good example be given by mercenary, greedy, depraved, and idle persons who only visit the village in order to insult, to despoil, and to terrorize? Olga remembered the pitiful, humiliated look of the old people when in the winter [one of them] had been taken to be flogged.

Two years later, as we shall see in *In the Ravine*, Chekhov will be far more radical in his attack on authority.

Did no one notice the effect of this frantic activity on his health? In March 1897 he dined with Suvorin at the Hermitage, where there was a convention of theater workers. Just before the dinner, blood started pouring from his mouth and over his short beard. The doctor rushed him to a clinic and discovered—as Chekhov himself pointed out—that the hemorrhage came from his right lung. He was kept at the clinic for more than two weeks and to Suvorin he made a literary joke: "The author of 'Ward No. 6' has been moved from Ward No. 16 to Ward No. 14."

He was plagued by visitors, he said, who came to see him two at a time, each one begging him not to speak and at the same time pestering him with questions. The worst was Tolstoy, who did not stop talking about himself for four hours. The incurable egotist said he had given up writing *Resurrection* and had started a long book, clearing up, once and for all, the question of Art. An addict of documentation, he said he had so far read sixty books on the subject. Tolstoy's thinking is not new, Chekhov wrote; wise men have always sung this song in a variety of tunes.

Old men have always been prone to see the end of the world, and have always declared that morality was degenerating to the uttermost point, and that Art was growing shallow and wearing thin, that people were growing feebler. . . .

Mellifluous and tactless, Tolstoy talked about life after death:

> He holds that all of us (people and animals) will live
> in a principle (reason, love), the essence and purpose
> of which is a mystery to us. To me this principle or
> force presents itself as a formless jelly-like mass. . . . my
> individuality . . . will be fused with this mass—such
> immortality I don't need, I don't understand it.

Tolstoy's visit provoked another hemorrhage. The doctor's
orders were severe. No more drinking or smoking. No more
farming: he must give up his medical work for good. He
must never again spend his winters in Melikhovo but must
go south to Nice and join the rest of the European
consumptives.

His brother Ivan took him by train to Melikhovo. Chekhov told his friends he was fairly well and only coughed
in the mornings, but he did have migraines and there was
trouble with his left eye. All the same, he was trying to pass
as a man of twenty-eight, with some success, "because I buy
expensive neckties and use Vera Violetta scent." He has
given up active work on the farm and does no more than
prune roses and feed sparrows and talks of going to Egypt
or to Sochi. At home they are cramming him with food but
he does not put on weight. He has still got the building of
two more schools on his hands, and he is fussing with his
brother Alexander's scheme of establishing a clinic for al-
coholics. (The generous Suvorin was one of those who sub-
scribed money to help this cause.) There, in his little hut

on the estate—Chekhov put up a flag there when he was ready to receive guests—he was still in trouble with the censor about *The Peasants* and had to make further cuts in *The Seagull*.

Scores of guests poured in without mercy: Chekhov could not resist inviting them and his sister could not hold them off. One or two unscrupulous people stayed for weeks, brought their families, treating the place as a pension. His brother Alexander even had the nerve to send his two noisy sons down for the holidays.

To get away from the guests and against the doctor's advice, Chekhov escaped secretly to Moscow for a night or two to see Lika Mizinova, who, like his Nina in *The Seagull*, had "shown stamina," and had recovered from her folly. At last, when the summer came, he took the advice of the doctors—but after his own fashion: he went south, but via Paris, where he stayed a day or two with the Suvorins and went to the Moulin Rouge once more and saw the *danse du ventre*, and afterwards to Biarritz, where he took French lessons with a pretty French girl who promised to come to visit him later in Nice but who didn't turn up. Biarritz delighted him. One seems to see the flashy necktie of the complete tourist as he sits on the *plage* and listens to the voice of the Bay of Biscay that "roars even on a calm day." The bracing fashionable resort was full of instantly detectable and boring Russians. There were letters from Lika and he returned to his game with her.

All day I sit in the sun and think of you and why you love to write about lopsided things and I've decided

. . . that your own sides are a bit wonky. You want people to realize this and find you attractive.

He loved her letters: "I value not only *Reinheit* in women, but also kindness."

Then, in September, the Atlantic rain blew in and he got off at last to Nice and found a cheap room in the Pension Russe, 70 francs all in, and it had carpets everywhere—his Balzac-like passion—and a bed "like Cleopatra's."

Culture juts out of every shop window, every wicker basket, every dog smells of civilization.

The pension was always full of a mixed lot of bickering Russian ladies. He could not speak French but he could read it after a fashion. He was reading Voltaire.

He loved Nice and its cafés, its street noises, and the musicians who played under his windows. He liked the French égalité. The only bore was the mosquitoes, he said, "but I passionately love the sun." Later, in December, he was spitting blood again. It wasn't serious, but he found going upstairs exhausting. He wrote one or two slight stories: the famous *Pecheneg*, about the old Cossack officer (we have heard of him before in *The Steppe*) who had brought up his children as savages (they threw chickens into the air and shot them) and who bored his guests with his theories about the Golden Age. Then there is *On the Cart*, about the misery of a girl teaching in a rural school at Melikhovo— stories that came from his memory:

I have never written directly from Nature. I have let my memory sift the subject, so that only what is important or typical is left in it as in a filter.

In January 1898 he read in the French papers that Émile Zola was being prosecuted for libel in his famous letter *J'accuse*. The attack on Zola in the conservative Russian press, especially in Suvorin's paper *New Time*, infuriated Chekhov. He set about a thorough study of the Dreyfus case and protested fiercely to the aging Suvorin, who was, after all, the proprietor if not now the editor:

> You write [he wrote to Suvorin] that *you* are annoyed with Zola. Here everyone feels as though a new, better Zola has arisen. In his trial he has been cleansed as though in turpentine from grease-spots, and now shines before the French in his true brilliance. There is a purity and moral elevation that was not suspected in him. You should follow the whole scandal from the beginning.

He went on to write that

> a brew has been gradually concocted on the basis of anti-Semitism, a principle reeking of the slaughter-house. When something is wrong with us we seek the cause outside ourselves . . . capitalism, the Masons, the Syndicate, the Jesuits—all phantoms, but how they do relieve our anxieties!

He reminded Suvorin of Dr. Fyodor Haas, who in the previous generation had spent his personal income on prison reform; of Korolenko, who saved the Multans from forced labor—a Finnish-speaking people, resident in the Russian Empire, who had been falsely accused of making sacrifices to pagan gods. Yes, Chekhov agreed, Zola was not Voltaire, "nor are any of us Voltaires, but there comes a time when not being a Voltaire is as irrelevant as can be."

Chekhov had read the stenographic notes of Zola's trial. He wrote to his brother Alexander, who was now employed by *New Time*, that the paper had behaved abominably:

> The old man and I have exchanged letters on the subject (in a tone of great moderation, however), and have both dropped the subject. I don't want to write and I don't want his letters in which he keeps justifying the tactlessness of his paper by saying he loves the military.

Was there a break with Suvorin after this protest? Many of Chekhov's friends hoped for it. But no. Chekhov knew how generous Suvorin had been with financial help for his school building at Melikhovo. On the other hand, he did say that "the old man," who was now in his sixties, had left the running of his paper to his reactionary young sons.

More seriously, at the beginning of 1899 there was a students' strike in Petersburg on the anniversary of the foundation of the university. The new generation of students were radicals and the new Tsar had turned out to be more reactionary than his predecessor. The police were called in to disperse the students in Moscow, to which the rioting had spread, and there was a threat of forcing them into military service. Suvorin's paper supported the authorities and was boycotted by the students. Chekhov told his brother Alexander that he was sorry for the old man: "but I'm not at all sorry for those who are surrounding him." There had long been a rumor that the paper had taken a subsidy from the government and the French General Staff. Suvorin was called upon to appear at a "Court of Honor" by a writers' committee known as the Self-Aid Committee. Suvorin refused and Chekhov supported him in this.

> In an Asiatic country, where freedom of the press and freedom of conscience do not exist, where the government and nine-tenths of society look upon a journalist as an enemy, where life is so cramped and vile, where there is little hope of better times—in such a country amusements like pouring slops on one another in Courts of Honor etc. put writers in the ridiculous and pathetic position of little caged animals biting each other's tails off.

He warned Suvorin about his politics: "Drive nature out of the door and she'll fly in by the window." And when Suvorin's wife reproached Chekhov for not coming strongly forward in defence of his generous benefactor and friend, he said:

> Whatever people are saying now they have been saying for a long time everywhere, and you and your husband did not know the truth, as kings do not know the truth.

Chekhov told his friends he liked Suvorin very much but that he had "never known a man so irresolute and lacking in character."

Chekhov's friends were noticing that, whatever he said about his health, he had aged. His beard was turning gray and behind the glasses of his pince-nez his eyes were narrower; his smile was dim and his jokes were few. In Nice the painter Braz made a second attempt at painting his portrait, and indeed it is the picture of a melancholy and defeated man. Chekhov wrote: "If I have become a pessimist and write gloomy tales then the fault is in this portrait of me."

He was getting tired of Nice and wanted to get back to Melikhovo. Euphoria and desperation alternate in the classical condition of the consumptive. He falls back on the reckless optimism and the skills of his affections. Skills? He was still pursued by the relentless Lydia Avilova and eventually hit upon the solution of diverting her by getting her to hunt through magazines for copies of his early stories, which he had lost, so that he could revise them for a collected edition of his works. She eagerly agreed. It was a strange cure but it seemed to calm her. It is again noticeable that he still had the art of turning his half-love-affairs into friendships. Once more we have to suppose that his sexual temperature was low.

Chapter Fourteen

Chekhov at last surrendered to his doctors and agreed that he must now spend every winter in the Crimea at Yalta. Before he left he had seen Stanislavsky and Nemirovich-Danchenko, who had recently founded the Moscow Art Theater and were anxious to include *The Seagull* in the repertoire of their first season. The earlier failure of the play still embittered Chekhov but he gave in. He mistrusted Stanislavsky and his literal realism, especially his taste for banal "noises off"—the croaking of frogs, the chirping of grasshoppers and the barking of dogs. One of the actors told him that Stanislavsky wanted to bring in a crying baby among the servants who come to say good-bye to Arkadina at the end of the play. All the same, public hostility to *The Seagull* had gone. The following year when he left Yalta on a short defiant trip and went back to Moscow, the company put on a private performance for him "without the stage sets," and he complained. He said that he could not judge the play dispassionately. He said the actress who played Nina gave an abominable performance, sobbing violently: that Trigorin walked and talked like a paralytic without "a will

of his own." Still, he did say honestly that the play gripped
him "so that I could hardly believe it was I who had written
it." In spite of his "war with the bacilli," he did not want
to leave Moscow. He was very excited by the revival of his
play.

> Lovely actresses! If I'd stayed on any longer I should
> have lost my head. The older I get, the faster and
> stronger does the pulse of life beat in me.

The play was now an enormous success.

In his rooms at Yalta in 1898 Chekhov said he felt "locked
in." Patriotically, he said the little resort was more agreeable
and cleaner than Nice. The warmth of the sea, the mountains
and especially the flowers delighted him, though he found
the leaves of the southern trees metallic. The claims of Yalta
to be the cultural capital of the Crimea were absurd. Fame
in Petersburg or Moscow was an excitement: one kept to
one's set. But in Yalta the public thought they owned you
personally and you were on duty for tedious chats in the
street or sudden callers. He was not a man to say no, and
he soon found himself elected as a trustee of the girls' sec-
ondary school and going into the question of building a
new sanatorium for the population of consumptives and—
of all minor annoyances—becoming a kind of estate agent.
Doctors in Moscow plagued him for addresses where they
could send their patients.

The railway had not yet reached the town. To leave one
had to take the steamer to Sevastopol and drive over the
mountains to the nearest railway station. Books took weeks

to arrive; the mail was erratic. He remembered that years before in Yalta he had written *A Dreary Story*, which had established his fame as a writer. Now he knew he had matured and was free to look back. We find him telling a correspondent that the lazy man has time for listening to more people than the man who sticks to his desk all day, who "hears little" and is really shut up in a shell.

Listening is Chekhov's impulse in the three new stories he is now working on. They are linked stories of remembering: *The Man in a Case*, *Gooseberries* and *About Love*, in which the talkers will talk of love "in the Russian fashion." We have heard this kind of declamation in *Ariadne*; now Chekhov frames these three stories so that they will be a series. We see two friends on a shooting holiday in the country, sleeping rough, in a barn, and telling their stories in the evening. Burkin, the schoolmaster in *The Man in a Case*, tells about a former colleague of his, Belikov, a teacher of Greek. He is distinctly a character of Gogolian absurdity. He is a petty tyrant, a frightened bachelor who hates all innovation, all pleasure, and above all fears the dangers of freedom; he has a terror of "repercussions" and worships official edicts. He is compared to a hermit crab:

> His great feat was to sport galoshes and an umbrella even on the finest days and he always wore a warm padded greatcoat. He kept his umbrella in a holder, his watch in a gray chamois-leather bag.

All the masters at the school, including the headmaster himself, unite in an intrigue to get Belikov married. They find a hearty, shouting Ukrainian girl who cannot stop laughing. They might have succeeded, but unfortunately Belikov sees she has gone recklessly in for the new, morally subversive craze for bicycling. There had been signs, up till then, that he was attracted to her, but now he goes to the length of protesting to her brother, who is also a cyclist, and threatens to protest to the authorities. In an angry scene the brother pushes him downstairs. Belikov is broken. His health goes. He dies, and the Ukrainian girl bursts into tears at his funeral. "Ukrainian girls can only cry or laugh," says the narrator. "They have no intermediate mood." Still, "it's a great pleasure, frankly, burying a Belikov." But, the storyteller adds, "what a lot of other such encapsulated people remain, and what a lot of them the future holds in store!"

The next story, *Gooseberries*, is told by the veterinary surgeon. The sportsmen are soaked by rain and are given shelter by an old friend, Alyokhin, who slaves in his fields. He stops work to lead them to his handsome manor. He himself works so hard that he has not washed for months. He takes them first to his millpond. The water looks filthy—"cold, muddy and malignant"—but the veterinarian dives in. We see water lilies rock as he goes to the bottom again and again and comes up crying out, "Oh my goodness, oh Lord have mercy on me!" as he floats to enjoy the rain pouring onto his face. At the house they all clean up and go to Alyokhin's elegant drawing room, where they see his beautiful servant Pelageya. The veterinarian then tells the story of his brother, a civil servant. He married a rich widow, who soon conveniently died and left him all her money, after which he bought an estate in the country. He has become self-indulgent and gluttonous, especially of the irresistible gooseberries he has cultivated. He believes that the peasants, whom he corrupts with kegs of vodka, love him because he calls himself a gentleman. The veterinarian warns his friends about the deceits of country bliss and comfort. He says:

> "Evidently the happy man only feels at ease because the unhappy bear their burdens in silence, and without that silence happiness would be impossible. . . . There ought to be behind the door of every happy, contented man someone standing with a hammer continually reminding him with a tap that there are unhappy people; that . . . life will show him her claws sooner or later, trouble will come for him."

Then Alyokhin tells the final story, *About Love*. It begins with a reference to Pelageya, the beautiful and graceful servant, who is in love with the bestial cook, a man who is fanatically religious and a drunk, and who beats her. She had not wanted to marry but simply wanted to live with him, which his religion forbade.

> "How love is born [says Alyokhin], why Pelageya does not love somebody more like herself in her spiritual and external qualities, and why she fell in love with Nikanor, that ugly snout . . . how far questions of personal happiness are of consequence in love—all that is unknown. . . . We Russians of the educated class have a partiality for these questions that remain unanswered."

Alyokhin's own story is not of stormy attractions. It is simple and sad. He had become a close friend of a neighboring couple, a judge and his wife, who have been more than generous to him. He was a constant visitor. The result was that he and the judge's wife slowly fell in love, without admitting it to each other or disturbing the husband. They were often alone together. This unacknowledged love went on for years.

> "Anna Alekseyevna and I used to go to the theater together, always walking there; we used to sit side by side in the stalls, our shoulders touching. I would take the opera glass from her hand without a word, and feel . . . that we could not live without each other. . . . When we came out of the theater we always said goodbye and parted as though we were strangers. Goodness knows what people were saying about us in the town already, but there was not a word of truth in it all."

Years go by and in time Anna becomes irritable; she is becoming ill. "If I dropped anything, she would say coldly 'I congratulate you.'"

One evening when he is dining with the family Alyokhin bursts out with indignation about a political scandal. Four Jews have been falsely charged with incendiarism in some town or other. The wife appeals to her husband, the judge, and asks how such a thing could happen. The judge is one of those simpleminded men who firmly believe that once a man is charged before a court he is guilty, that doubt about guilt can only be expressed in legal form on paper. Certainly not at a private dinner. "You and I did not set fire to the place," he explains gently to his wife, "and you see we are not condemned and not put in prison." In short, the judge, his wife and indeed Alyokhin are as much "encased" as the grotesque Belikov was.

The judge is transferred to a distant province, and his wife follows later. Alyokhin joins the large crowd who go to the station to see her off. At the last moment he dashes into her compartment and they both declare their feelings as they part. And here we see a variation of Chekhov's classic good-byes. The train moves off; Alyokhin escapes alone to the empty compartment next door and sits weeping and gets off at the next station. At that moment (Alyokhin tells his friends) he "understood that when you love you must either, in your reasonings about that love, start from what is highest, from what is more important than happiness or unhappiness, sin or virtue in their accepted meaning, or you must not reason at all."

The rain has stopped, the sun comes out, the schoolmaster and the veterinarian leave the handsome drawing room, where the family portraits have seemed to be alive and even listening to the talkers. The sportsmen gaze at the garden and the millpond, which is no longer dark and malignant but shines like a mirror. They think of the sorrow that must have been on Anna's face when Alyokhin declared his love too late. In the last line of the story she comes doubly to life:

Both of them had met her in the town, and Burkin knew her and thought her beautiful.

For Chekhov the story had an exasperating consequence. Lydia Avilova wrote to him that it portrayed her and an incident in their imaginary romance. The clinching fact was that he had once put her and her children on a train some- where. Chekhov did his best to disillusion her and their exchange of letters was tart. Nevertheless, after his death she went back to romanticizing a love affair which had not existed.

Chekhov did not continue with the conversational series. He had tired of his talkers. To talk of love in this fashion was a too comfortable, too wistful, even generalizing, device, too close to the manner of Turgenev. His best stories are not safely framed: they are direct and open. He was mature enough to say good-bye to good-byes. If in early life he had been evasive, now, in middle life, he is willing to see love as a continuing gift, surviving its difficulties. In the delight- ful, well-known *The Darling* there is no need of discussion. The simple heroine is a woman who loves by nature, cannot think or speak for herself, but instinctively echoes the opin- ions of a husband. If he ignores or tricks her, she will adopt his worries or interests as if they were hers. When he runs a puppet show and the public is driven off by bad weather, she groans with him at his failures as if they were hers. When he dies she will take up with a timber merchant and her talk will be about the terrible anxieties of the timber trade. If she is deserted she will look for someone else whose miseries she can take over. At the famous end of the story, when there is no man left, she takes over a small boy who is not her son and gives herself to all his troubles in his lessons, learns them herself and denounces the schools for making the boy's life a misery. A simpleton, a mindless fool, a comic echo without personality or interests? Is she without will? No, she is no one unless she loves. It is not a matter of charity, nor of subservience or possessive nullity. It is not even a talent. Without loving she has no self. Tolstoy admired this story more than any other Chekhov had written and, of course, imposed his own theories on it in a well-known introduction.

Chapter Fifteen

Chekhov was bored at Yalta and was tired of living in two rooms as a lodger, of going every day for his meals to the little restaurants of the town. He was bored with food and drifted into eating less and less. Local acquaintances told him he ought to buy a house, but he was not rich. He was supporting his parents at Melikhovo and in his letters he is still talking about his debts! There is an expansive Balzac in Chekhov's nature. For the moment, he buys a cheap cottage of two or three rooms in the mountains outside the town, on the excuse that his parents and sister can stay there if they come to see him. He was never to live there. The early improvement in his health did not last: his other lung was now infected. Presently a dramatic event changed his situation. A garbled telegram arrived at the post office, undelivered because it was misaddressed. "All Yalta" knew what it said before he did. The proud and seemingly immortal tyrant Pavel had suffered a rupture while lifting a heavy box of his son's books at Melikhovo. He had been rushed to a Moscow clinic and had died. Chekhov's first words were "If I had been there to operate I could have saved his life." He saw at once that his mother could not stay at Melikhovo alone. His sister was there only at weekends because she was still teaching in Moscow. In any family crisis Anton had always taken his mother's part and now he at once resumed his responsibility as head of the family. It was clear that Melikhovo must be sold, that his mother and sister must come to Yalta and live with him. Responsibility renewed his will. Where would he put his mother? Not in lodgings. He was tired of lodgings. He must get a house. Rent it? No. Melikhovo must be sold, and he would build a house in Yalta and so provide for his mother and sister, after his own death.

Chekhov stuck to his independence. Money? His only hope lay in pressing Suvorin to hurry with a complete edition of all his stories. The proposal had been made long ago but was languishing, for the old man had left his business in the hands of his negligent sons, who were uninterested in complete editions and, in any case, were slow payers. Indeed they owed Chekhov five thousand rubles and payment was overdue. Reluctantly, Suvorin's sons offered him twenty thousand rubles. While he was considering this he heard that a new publisher called Marx had just published Tolstoy's *Resurrection* on generous terms, and Tolstoy had recommended that he go to Marx, who had the reputation of being sharp and cunning but who paid well. Unlike Surorin's books, which were cheap and unattractive and intended for the mass market, Marx's editions were elegantly bound and were well printed on decent paper. When Marx heard of Chekhov's dilemma he at once offered him thirty thousand rubles, to be paid in installments. Chekhov consulted Suvorin, who pointed out the flaw in the offer. Marx was tricking him. He was proposing to buy outright all Chekhov's copyrights, past, present and future. Chekhov's level-headed sister agreed with Suvorin. She said *she* would take charge of his contracts, just as the Countess Tolstoy had so successfully done in defense of her children's future when Tolstoy had renounced his royalties on ethical grounds. Like all authors, Chekhov knew, at heart, that the outright sale of copyrights was a folly, but he brushed that aside. His response was to push Marx's offer up to seventy-five thousand, but he did refuse, happily, to include the copyrights on his plays and on all new works as published in periodicals. The contract was signed and he made one of his jokes: "I am a Marxist now."

Suvorin said Chekhov would regret his decision, and indeed it was not long before he did. For years Marx made a fortune at Chekhov's expense. Suvorin also said that he knew what would happen when Chekhov received his first installment: Chekhov would simply increase his charities. He did. He immediately gave away five thousand rubles as a contribution to the building of a new school on the outskirts of Yalta and one thousand rubles to his brother Alexander, who had at last given up drinking and needed the money to buy a new house. Anton also gave money for the education of the daughter of a needy man who had once slaved as underpaid apprentice at Chekhov's side in his father's shop at Taganrog.

Now Chekhov started looking for a site for a house in Yalta for his mother, his sister and himself. He was soon deep in mortgaging, for the sale of Melikhovo, which his sister was managing, took longer than he had hoped. There was a pause, during which he was looking for a site and finding a young and enterprising architect of sufficient originality, for he was eager to build a house that would be modern, original and a credit to the town. He was indeed building what would become his monument. His sister came down at last to see and approve the site. She was shocked at first when she was taken to a stretch of wasteland covered with scrub on the outskirts of the town: it had attracted Chekhov because the garden adjoined a Tatar cemetery. (As we know from his trip to Genoa and from the two moonlight scenes in the story *Ionych*, he had a poet's response to cemeteries. Was not every grave a complete story or life history?) A Tatar funeral was taking place when he and his sister got there, and she was depressed by this ominous incident, but when they went back to his lodgings they were soon excited and laughing over his plans and his talk of the roses he would grow there, which would outdo the roses of Melikhovo. He wrote to his brother Mikhail, still pretending that the house was simply for the winter:

> Nothing will be needed apart from the house, no outbuildings of any sort; it will all be under one roof. The coal, wood and everything will be in the basement. The hens lay the whole year round, and no special house is needed for them.

It was some time before Melikhovo was sold and the new house could be built and made fit for his mother and sister to live in. In the meantime he had moved them into a more comfortable flat in Moscow, where he could stay if he took a trip to the city. Meanwhile his health was deteriorating: he had little sleep at night and he could eat little. Still, there were good days in which, with the help of a Turkish gardener, he turned his little garden into a paradise of new trees and flowers. They made a pool, which was soon inhabited by frogs and, he said, "other crocodile-like creatures." Two stray dogs had adopted him and also a crane, which followed him around. On the bad days he had prolonged headaches, when he could not work, and visitors noticed that he would stuff a bloodstained hankerchief into his pocket.

If the contract with Marx was dubious it had one benefit. In the first six months he had reread, corrected and judged a lifetime's stories for the complete edition. Much of his early work had been done in a hurry: now he had to cut, tighten or reject. In his later work he had been alert to the false image or sentence. The danger—as we know from Henry James's revisions—lay in the temptation to elaborate, but Chekhov was a cutter, sensitive to the musicality of simple language.

When, at last, Chekhov moved into his new house, which was far from being finished, he was alarmed to see how fast the installments of his contract with Marx melted away. He was cheered by the news that an old play of his, *Uncle Vanya*, had been successfully revived and played on tour in the provinces, but he told Gorky that he had given up the theater for good and was going back to writing nothing but stories. Rereading his own work had revived his imagination. He would soon be writing *The Lady with the Little Dog* and two of his surpassing masterpieces: *In the Ravine* and, above all, *The Bishop*.

We must go back a year to September 1898, when Chekhov was still at Melikhovo and had gone to Moscow and had seen the rehearsals of the new production of *The Seagull*. He was struck by the beauty and acting of Olga Knipper, who played the part of Irina. He wrote to Suvorin that her voice, her nobility and warmth were superb: "I felt choked with emotion. If I had stayed in Moscow I would have fallen in love with this Irina." In the following year, when he had risked another trip to Moscow, he saw Olga again and took her to an exhibition of Levitan's pictures. He met her family, who had relatives known to him in Yalta, and she had been brought by his sister to stay at Melikhovo. Olga's father was an engineer of Alsatian origin, now working in Moscow. Her mother was Russian and a talented musician. Olga was going off on holiday to the Caucasus with her brother and Chekhov begged her to visit him in Yalta on her way back. At the age of thirty-eight he had fallen seriously in love. He wrote to her and she did not answer.

> What does this mean? [he wrote]. Where are you? You are so stubborn in not sending news of yourself that . . . we are already thinking you have forgotten us and have got married in the Caucasus. . . . The author is forgotten—how terrible, how cruel, how perfidious!

She was ten years younger than himself.

She replied that his letters had made her "burst out laughing with joy." He wrote again, arranging to meet her on her journey back from Batum and take her back to Yalta. She came and, very properly, stayed with the family of his doctor, and Chekhov stayed in an hotel near the harbor. Only one wing of his new house was finished, and she was depressed. She was worried about his health. She noticed that he never had regular meals, that he looked neglected and was soon tired. Although they met every day, she could rarely persuade him to have dinner with her at the doctor's. He went back to Moscow with her, where she had a part in a new play, and they drove by carriage together on a memorable journey across the mountains. Their friendship warmed. It was not until the following summer that she came to Yalta again, when his mother and sister were in the house. By now Chekhov and Knipper were lovers.

Now he bursts out in a letter to her. She is his "precious, unusual actress," his "wonderful woman," and

if you only knew how happy your letter made me! I bow down before you, bow low, so low that my forehead is touching the bottom of my well, which has today been dug to a depth of sixty feet. I have got used to you and miss you. . . .

And then comes one of his evasive fantasies:

If Nadenka only knew what is going on in my soul there would be quite a scandal.

("Nadenka" was Chekhov's imaginary jealous wife or fiancée.)

There is no doubt that Chekhov's passion was serious. Before he met Olga he had written to his brother Mikhail, who was thinking of getting married:

> What am I to say? To marry is interesting only for love; to marry a girl simply because she is nice is like buying something one does not want at a bazaar solely because it is of good quality.
>
> The most important rivet in family life is love, sexual attraction. . . . all the rest is unreliable and dreary, however cleverly we make our calculations. So you see, what's needed isn't a nice girl but one you love. No mean obstacle, that you'll agree.

Now, alone in Yalta, Chekhov writes what was to become the best-known of his love stories, *The Lady with the Little Dog*, in which a chance love affair takes possession of two people and changes them against their will, and which closes with them far apart and rarely able to meet. Their fervor for each other grows with every new good-bye. If the story seems to evoke aspects of Chekhov's meetings with Olga Knipper, it is transferred to a couple totally unlike them. In *The Lady with the Little Dog*, Gurov and Anna are both married. He works in a bank in Moscow, Anna lives in a dead provincial town called S—, a town which will reappear in *The Three Sisters*. Each has gone on a stolen holiday to Yalta, a resort notorious for its casual love affairs. Gurov is an experienced forty-year-old amorist who has a stern wife.

Anna is married to a dull provincial civil servant. She is ten years younger than her husband. The opening sentence of the story dryly establishes the inciting spell of holiday gossip.

It was said that a new person had appeared on the sea front: a lady with a little dog.

This at once stirs the hunting instinct of the experienced Gurov. He sees her, "the new person," sitting near him in an open-air restaurant. Her dog growls at him and he shakes his finger at it. He has seen at once that she is pretty, naïve and "angular" in her gestures. She marvels when he tells her that he has an arts degree and has been trained to be an opera singer, but had given it up to work in a bank. She tells him, in her awkward way, that her husband is some sort of official.

In Yalta the only exciting event of the day is the arrival of the evening steamboat. She says she is expecting a friend. They join the crowd at the harbor and he notices that Anna is pretending to look at the disembarking passengers for her "friend." They wait on the quayside until the crowd has dispersed and dusk creeps up on the couple standing alone. He suggests they go for a drive along the coast. She does not answer. He kisses her and whispers, "Let us go to your room." Silently she agrees. Her room is lit by a single candle and smells of the scent she had bought the day before at a Japanese shop. Gurov thinks, "What encounters one does have in life." He had known "carefree, good-natured women, happy in their love and grateful for happiness, however brief." He had also known women

like his wife who loved insincerely, with idle chatter, affectedly, hysterically, with an expression suggesting that this was neither love nor passion, but something more significant.

In others he had glimpsed a rapacity, a wanting more from life than it could give, and these were

unreflecting, domineering, unintelligent women . . . not in their first youth, and when Gurov grew cold to them their beauty excited his hatred, and the lace on their underclothes seemed to him like scales.

We shall not see the seduction. Unlike later novelists, Chekhov never describes the sexual act: Russian manners and especially the censor would not have allowed such scenes. We shall know the seduction has occurred only by the look of consternation on Anna's face,

as though someone had suddenly knocked at the door. She had her own special view—a very serious one—of what had happened. She thought of it as her "downfall," it seemed, which was all very strange and inappropriate.

"It's wrong," she says, and adds the hackneyed words, "You will be the first to despise me now." The nonplussed

Gurov cuts himself a slice of a watermelon which is on the table and for a silent half hour "eats without haste." (Yes, we think, that is the point so many novelists have missed: a seduction stuns.) She begins to sob, "God forgive me, it's awful," and breaks into banal confessions of guilt, how she had wanted, for once, "to live, to live!" She has been mad and dazed in Yalta and lied when she had told her husband—whom she calls a "flunkey"—that she was going away because she was ill. Gurov calms her and at last they both begin laughing. They eventually go for a long drive to Oreanda along the beautiful coast, and we hear that her husband's grandfather was a German but her husband is Orthodox Russian—oddly close to Olga Knipper's origins.

At Oreanda they sit by the shore and listen to the monotonous, conniving, breaking of the sea. One remembers the sea breaking in *The Duel*. For Gurov it is a symbol of the mystery of an eternity that seems to both enlarge and dwarf us. (In his *Notebooks* Chekhov had written one of his gnomic phrases: "It seems to me: the sea and myself.") The couple sit a little apart on a bench and are silent. Gurov is thinking:

[E]verything is beautiful in this world—everything except what we think or do ourselves when we forget the higher aims of existence and our human dignity.

True or untrue? Gurov, the experienced seducer, is changing.

The couple part: he to Moscow, she to the town of S—.

For Gurov the affair seems simply one more conquest, yet he finds Anna haunts him. To relieve the seriousness of the tale, Gurov is seen about to confide what has happened to a man at his club, but the man mishears him and thinks he is talking about the sturgeon they had just eaten. Gurov is surprised and disappointed that he does not dream of Anna. He now looks at other women, thinking for a moment to find her in them. He cannot rid himself of her image. This might be the end of many of Chekhov's earlier love stories but now he wants it to grow, and we shall see Gurov driven to unforgettable pursuit. He is impelled to go to S——, and does so, telling his wife that he has to go to St. Petersburg on some errand. There he finds Anna's house. It is ominously surrounded by a long gray fence, studded with nails, a symbol of the inaccessible "prison" in which she has had to live since her marriage. The sound of a piano being played suggests she and her husband may be there. He catches sight of her dog being let out into the garden by a housekeeper and he has the impulse to call it, but he is in such fear and confusion that he has forgotten the dog's name. He returns to his hotel and is desperate until he sees a poster saying that *The Geisha* is opening the following night at the local theater—an occasion when she, her husband and all official people are likely to be there. Now the story changes key.

Gurov goes to the theater. There she is, "this little woman, in no way remarkable," clutching the "vulgar lorgnette in her hand," and there also is her tall, obsequious husband, wearing an order on his uniform, and it does indeed look like a waiter's number. Gurov sits there through the first act; then at the interval the husband goes out to smoke. Thinking that all eyes in the audience are on him, Gurov goes over to speak to Anna. He can hardly speak, nor can she, and she stares in terror at him. She rushes out of the auditorium and he follows her into the drafty corridor. Their love becomes theater within theater. A cold stale wind seems to blow as she races past vulgar crowds of officials in uniforms "legal, scholastic and civil," past ladies, past fur coats swaying on their pegs as they rush by, down stairs and passages, until at last he catches up with her, breathless, under a balcony. A Chekhovian detail: two bored schoolboys who are smoking cigarettes look down to watch as Gurov takes Anna into his arms and kisses her and she clings to him. There the lovers stand, dazed, almost speechless, in the buzz of chatter and the sound of the meaningless tuning up of the orchestra. She gasps out a promise to find an excuse for coming to Moscow to see him. And so they part and he leaves the theater.

Remember that we have seen the story through Gurov's eyes and that Chekhov's intention is to show him as a maturing and feeling man arguing with himself about the unexpected situation. The scene requires a momentary point of ironic distraction. It happens that Gurov has to drop his little daughter at her school on the way to his secret rendezvous, and as they walk the child asks her father why the pavements are still slushy after the sleet storm in the night. Gurov tells her kindly: "It is three degrees above zero, and yet it is sleeting. . . . The thaw is only on the surface of the earth; there is quite a different temperature in the upper strata of the atmosphere."

The child chatters on: "And is there no thunder in the winter, Daddy?"

He explains that too. When he has dropped the child at her school he is free to reflect on his two lives, full of stereotyped truths and untruths.

> Everything . . . in which he was sincere and did not deceive himself, everything that made the kernel of his life, was hidden from other people.

The real subject of the story is this serious conflict in the minds of the lovers. At the hotel they are in each other's arms and their theories vanish. Every two or three months after this they will meet and wrestle with their dilemma.

> [They] could not understand why he had a wife and she a husband. . . . They forgave each other for what they were ashamed of in their past, they forgave everything in the present, and felt that this love of theirs had changed them both. . . . And it seemed as though in a little while the solution would be found, and then a new and splendid life would begin.

And there Chekhov leaves them. As he once said, it is not the function of art to solve problems but to present them correctly.

In the year before writing *The Lady with the Little Dog* Chekhov had been entirely occupied with stories: *Ionych*, *The Darling*, *The New Dacha*, which echoes Misail's struggle with the peasants in *My Life*, and *On Official Duty*. The last is remarkable for its portrait of a country policeman who has to spend a wretched night during a blizzard with the body of a ruined landowner who has committed suicide, while the young magistrate wines and dines well in a country house. Tolstoy admired this story. Chekhov was eager to write a long story, the famous *In the Ravine*, but this had to be put aside. The Moscow Art Theater was pressing him for a new play. At Yalta he was ill, "torn up by the roots," he said, longing for Olga.

> I am torn up by the roots. . . . I don't drink though I am fond of drinking. I love noise and don't hear it. . . . I am in the condition of a transplanted tree which is hesitating whether to take root or to begin to wither.

All he can offer the Moscow Art Theater for the new season is an old play, *Uncle Vanya*, which has never been put on in Moscow.

Uncle Vanya has a curious history. It was extracted from an earlier play, *The Wood Demon*, which was much longer. Chekhov had written it when he was staying with the Lint-varyov family in the Ukraine.

The people and scene of the earlier play recall something Chekhov had said about life in the Ukraine:

> There are old neglected gardens and poetical estates, shut up and deserted, where dwell the souls of beautiful women.

In *Uncle Vanya* the scene is less seductive. The forests are being cut down in a haphazard way, the railway has crept in, factories have followed. We shall see a large half-neglected house with twenty-six rooms which is occupied by Uncle Vanya, who manages the estate, and his niece Sonya, who helps him with it. She actually owns the place, having inherited it from her mother. The profits, such as they are, go to support Sonya's father, an elderly, gouty, cantankerous professor of art who does not reside on the estate but who happens to be staying there with his young second wife, the beautiful Yelena. Other characters include Astrov, a local doctor, Telegin, an impoverished garrulous landowner, and the widowed Mariya Vasilyevna, mother of Vanya and of the professor's first wife.

Peace? We are about to see an absurd and acrimonious "month in the country" which will be very far from Turgenevan. The interrelationships are complicated, as they often are in country life. The play may strike us as being something of an intricate novel, but its popularity in the provinces even before it was revived by the Moscow Art Theater suggests that it had the spell of normal country gossip about "goings on." The professor has some of the disturbing egotism of the professor in *A Dreary Story*. His arrival puts everyone's back up, especially Uncle Vanya's, and, as in *The Seagull*, if very tentatively, there are "tons of love," but here open tippling is added. Uncle Vanya tipples and so does Dr. Astrov, and both make passes at Yelena, who is beginning to hate her exasperating elderly husband. The plain Sonya longs for Dr. Astrov, who is treating the professor. Astrov is one of Chekhov's strong if frustrated doctors and is close to him in that he is not only a doctor but also an active propagandist for the conservation of the forests. He hates having to treat the workers who have been injured by industrial accidents—a feeling, we suppose, Chekhov would not have shared. At the center of the play is Uncle Vanya's mad jealousy of the learned professor. If only, Uncle Vanya cries out, he had "had a normal life," he could have been "a Dostoyevsky or a Schopenhauer!"

The general situation comes to a head when the professor has the nerve to call together everyone in the house to appall them with the suggestion that the estate should be sold and the proceeds invested in securities. This is too much for Uncle Vanya. He announces that the professor cannot do this because the estate is not his to sell. It belongs to his daughter, Sonya. In any case, Uncle Vanya and Sonya have nowhere else to live. They have run the farm for twenty-five years. And so in a mad fit, Uncle Vanya gets a gun and fires two shots at the professor. They miss. This is too much for Yelena, who is tired of Uncle Vanya's drunken attempts to seduce her, and of the doctor's also. She forces the professor to give up his plans and leave. She has been disturbed by Dr. Astrov's insinuation that as a faithful wife she will soon tire of living with a cantankerous old scholar. She is frightened by the insinuation for she has been more impressed by Dr. Astrov than she cares to admit. Life in the country is out of date, dull and corrupting in its spell.

For all its mingling of angers and farce, *Uncle Vanya* is a very subtle, thoughtful and imaginative play. Chekhov has the art of showing us farce as inverted poetry. Uncle Vanya is absurd but we are drawn irresistibly to his side. The professor is ruthless because he is locked up in his conceit as a scholar. Dr. Astrov is angered by the passing of youth and its illusions but is passionately indignant at the fallen condition of the Russian peasant. He is also manly and shrewd. There is a good moment when, privately talking to Uncle Vanya after the absurd shooting scene, he comforts him, saying:

> In the whole district there have only been two decent, civilized people—you and I. But ten years or so of this contemptible parochial existence have dragged us down.

And then suddenly he turns to the attack and says to Uncle Vanya: "Give me back what you took." (He has detected that Uncle Vanya has stolen a bottle of morphia from his medicine chest.)

> If you really must put an end to yourself why don't you go to the woods and shoot yourself there. But do give me back my morphia or else there will be talk and suspicion or people might think I have given it to you. . . . It'll be quite enough to have to do your post mortem.

In the end we shall see Uncle Vanya and Sonya alone, doing the farm accounts while the impoverished landowner Telegin rambles on about the past and plays his guitar. Less happily, for it is too pretty and too touching, Sonya says:

We shall hear the angels, we shall see the heavens covered with stars like diamonds. We shall see all earthly evils, all our sufferings, vanish in the flood of mercy which will fill the whole world, and our life will become peaceful, gentle, sweet as a caress. I believe it. . . . We shall rest.

Chapter Sixteen

In 1899 the Academy of Sciences celebrated the hundredth anniversary of the birth of Pushkin by admitting writers as Honorary Members. Tolstoy and Chekhov were among the first to be honored (in January 1900) by this very conservative society of scholars. Chekhov was skeptical, in two minds about the scholarly embrace, and joked about the honor. It meant that he could not be arrested, would not have to get a special passport for foreign travel and would be free of the supervision of customs officials. He signed letters to his friends as "Academicus, Hereditary Honorary Academician." And he wrote to a friend that he was pleased, but

> I shall be even more gratified when I lose that title as the result of some misunderstanding. And a misunderstanding is bound to occur, because the learned Academicians are very much afraid that we shall shock them.

Two years later he resigned when Gorky's membership in the Academy was revoked.

Meanwhile he was writing *In the Ravine* for Gorky's Marxist paper *Life*. What astonishes us is that this long, richly crowded story—it runs to fifteen thousand words—should have come from him when his disease was worsening. He deepens his portraits of people, he absents himself and *becomes* them and lets them speak in their voices as they live out their passions.

In *The Peasants* he evoked a village which had not changed for centuries. In the new story the corruption comes from contact with the intruding factories. The story opens with what seems to be one of his jokes:

> The village of Ukleyevo lay in a ravine so that only the belfry and the chimneys of the calico-printing factories could be seen from the high road and the railway-station. When travelers asked what village this was, they were told: "That's the village where the deacon ate all the caviare at the funeral."

No joke at all. The young novelist Bunin told Chekhov later on that he knew of the grotesque incident and had seen the place. We expect a story like this to be a study done in stark black and white; in fact it subtly evokes the inconsequent yet decisive and sudden passions of its people. Those who worked in the factories could afford to eat and simply glutted themselves. The rest took their chances, stole or crowded round the back door of the local grocer's store and begged.

On many days the village lay invisible under a chemical mist which rose from the stream that had been poisoned by the factories. Fever was endemic. The factory owners had bribed the police to do nothing about the contamination. Tsybukin, the owner of the village store, is a dishonest trader who sells everything from provisions such as bad meat and poor-quality vodka to cattle, pigs and hides. He even manages to sell peasant women's bonnets for export as fashionable wear. Yet he has also the character and habits of a patriarch. His second wife—not from the village—has made a half-charitable man of him.

> As soon as she was installed . . . everything in the house brightened up, as though the windows had been newly glazed. . . . the tables were covered with snow-white cloths. . . . at dinner, instead of eating from a common bowl, each person had a plate.

The new wife is the soul of simple charity, and the old man astonishes everyone by allowing her to feed the beggars who crowd round the store at night. He has shrewdly married off one of his sons, who is deaf, to a domineering shrew called Aksinya. She is a frightening money-minded sensual predator. Now he finds a wife for his second son, Anisim, a gaudy, excitable fellow who has bettered himself by becoming a police detective. Tsybukin has charitably found a poor waif from a nearby town for him, a charwoman's daughter called Lipa, a child who has only just reached the legal age for marriage. The decisive theme of the story is Aksinya's jealous hatred of Lipa. At Lipa's wedding to Anisim, Aksinya throws herself into the orgy of drinking, guzzling and dancing, and dominates the wedding:

Aksinya had naïve gray eyes which rarely blinked and a naïve smile played continually on her face. And in those unblinking eyes, and in that little head on the long neck, and in her slenderness there was something snake-like. Dressed all in green except for the yellow bodice, smiling, she looked like a viper stretching itself, head uplifted, in the young rye, as it watches someone go past in the spring.

Anisim, the bridegroom detective, is a plausible liar, an exhibitionist, creating rumor and alarm. He boasts that he can spot stolen goods instantly anywhere and claims that the rise in crime is due to the decline of religious belief; he himself privately denies the existence of God. We shall soon see that he is passing false coinage and, in this, is the slave of a bigger crook than himself. A few weeks after the marriage the village will learn that he has been caught, tried and given penal servitude. As a patriarch defending his family, Tsybukin tries to get Anisim released by bribing the prison governor, offering him "a silver glass stand with a spout," inscribed with the words "The soul knows its right measure," and he is naïve enough to be surprised that the traditional remedy fails. Tsybukin will be worried for the rest of his life about the difficulty of deciding what coinage is genuine and what is false, not only in trade but in the heart. We see all this through the voices and general mind of the village: the people are at first proud of Anisim and even defend him for a time. Then they will forget him, as indeed his young wife, Lipa, does once she has borne his son. The child is her total delight—and old Tsybukin's also. She cannot stop watching the baby in his cradle. She often bows to him and says, "Good day, Nikifor Anisimych!" And then she rushes at him and kisses him and says the same thing again when she leaves the room. To her mother, who has come to work in the family kitchen, she often remarks: "Why do I love him so much, mamma? Why do I feel sorry for him? . . . Who is he? What is he like? As light as a little feather, as a little crumb. . . . I love him like a real person. . . ."

Tsybukin's delight is marred by his worry about having accepted some of Anisim's false coins. He confesses his complicity to Varvara, his charitable wife, and naïvely, to calm him, she tells him to make his will and to make the baby his heir.

We come to a scene of horror. Aksinya is jealous of Lipa because a piece of land, which she covets, has been willed to Lipa's child. One day Aksinya finds Lipa washing clothes in a tub of boiling water, screams that Lipa is the wife of a convict and throws a pail of boiling water over the baby, shouting, "You stole my land: now take that!" She rushes out into the garden shouting out to the gaping crowd, who have heard the screams, that Tsybukin is a bandit who has a store of false coins, and she starts pulling the clothes off the washing line and stamps on them. "What a wild woman!" the crowd says in admiration of the scene. "She has gone mad." It is perfect that her frightened, doltish husband comes out and picks up the washing and pegs it back on the line—a classic example of Chekhov's skill at "making it true" by anticlimax. Lipa takes the scalded baby to a hospital many miles away, and there it dies.

The finale of the story is so thronged with the conflicting voices of the people that the village itself—and not some orderly narrator—seems to be telling it out of the passions they all share.

We see Lipa's long walk back from the hospital, alone on the empty country road, carrying the dead baby in her arms, too simple, too stunned, to be frightened or to grieve. Chekhov is at one with all who travel alone. Dusk has come: we see the moon rise, hear the mysterious cowlike call of the bittern, the mocking cries of the cuckoos and the operatic nightingales, the croaking of frogs, all indifferent to human misery. Lipa is not broken. What sustains the simple Lipa is a naïve question: "Where is the baby's soul *now*?" She is at last given a lift by a couple of carters and asks them how long a soul remains on earth after death. The older carter says:

> "Who can tell? Ask Vavila here, he has been to school. Now they teach them everything." . . .
> Vavila stopped the horse and only then answered: "Nine days. My uncle Kirilla died and his soul lived in our hut thirteen days after."
> "How do you know?"
> "For thirteen days there was a knocking in the stove."

"Yours is not the worst of sorrows," the old man says. "Life is long, there will be good and bad to come, there will be everything. Great is Mother Russia." And he tells her that he had been to Siberia and walked back, and his wife died there. "I have had good as well as bad. . . . I would be glad to live another twenty years, so there has been more of the good than the bad." The young Gorky enormously admired this part of the story.

Lipa does not get back to Ukleyevo until sunrise and there she can cry at last. She realizes that she has no place in the house and Aksinya shouts at her: "What are you bellowing for?" At the funeral of the baby Aksinya is dressed up in new clothes and has powdered her face. The crowd of guests and priests eat as if they had not eaten for days and Lipa waits humbly at table. A detail:

> The priest, lifting his fork on which there was a salted mushroom, said to her: "Grieve not for the babe, for of such is the Kingdom of Heaven."

Three years pass. The tragedy has been assimilated into village history. Aksinya has triumphed. After the funeral she has driven her rival, Lipa, out of the house, and Lipa goes to live with her mother and earns her living working in the brickfields with the crowd of village women. The avaricious Aksinya has bought land and virtually owns the brickfield. She has become rich as the mistress of one of the mill owners. Everyone is afraid of her. Even at the post office the postmaster jumps to his feet and says: "I humbly beg you to be seated, Aksinya Abramovna." She also controls the shop and there is a rumor that she has driven Tsybukin out of the house and gives him nothing to eat. He spends his time sitting on a bench in the street, where he still fears to be caught for his connection with the false money. His frightened, muddle-minded wife can do nothing. The last we see of Lipa is in the evenings, marching home and singing with the crowd of workers from the brickfields. Like them she is "singing in a high voice . . . as though triumphant and ecstatic" because the long day is over and she can rest. We see her and her mother lagging behind in the crowd to bow to Tsybukin and give him a piece of pie before going on their way, and crossing themselves for a long time afterwards. Some people in the village are sorry for the old man; others say he deserved what has happened to him.

Powerful as the story is, it is all the more powerful for being a drama which is heard in the day-to-day voices of the people as they work in their poisoned valley and yet also talk out of their inherited imagination. How exactly Chekhov has caught Aksinya's nature when he notes the naïveté of the face of this snakelike and ruthless woman: the naïveté of uncontrollable sexuality incited by the pursuit of money. In his maturity Chekhov goes to the inborn "nature" of his people, not to their merely observable idiosyncrasies. Who would have suspected that poverty would have given Lipa, the simple waif, an inborn will? How admirable it is that Chekhov accepts all contradictions. How much more remarkable that in a story so powerful in its drama, he has avoided all theatrical rhetoric but has let life tell its own tale.

The story was acclaimed by most critics and Gorky wrote a long ecstatic essay on it and made an important point:

Chekhov has been reproached with having no philosophy. The reproach is absurd. . . . Ever more often our ears can catch in his stories the melancholy but severe and deserved reproach that men do not know how to live, but at the same time, his sympathy with all men glows even brighter.

The Moscow Art Theater was still pressing Chekhov for a new play but he was too ill to go to Moscow to discuss it with them and persuaded them to bring their company to the Crimea to put on performances of *The Seagull* and *Uncle Vanya*. Their success was sensational in Yalta and Sevastopol and there were exhausting festivities: the whole company swarmed in his new house. Olga for some time had been hinting at marriage. She found the gossip about their situation unpleasant. He calls her his sweet little actress, his wonderful Olga, the joy of his life, his delightful Knipperschitz, but she is determined on marriage.

I am tired of the game of hide and seek. I cannot bear to watch your mother's suffering. . . . It is awful. I feel as if I were between two fires at your place. Tell me what you think about it. . . . You never say anything—don't always dismiss everything as a joke. I can't help feeling you don't love me any more.

He points out that most of the year, when she was playing in Moscow or on tour, they would be as much apart if they were married. But she insists. At last he gives in.

If you will give me your word that not a single soul in Moscow will know of our wedding until it is over, I will marry you on the day of my arrival if you like. For some reason I have a fearful dread of the ceremony, the congratulations and the champagne which one has to hold in one's hand while smiling vaguely.

He had always hated being the center of public occasions; he loathed speeches. And, he told her, he had everything in order except one thing: his health. "Just as I'll be alone in my grave, so in essence I shall live alone."

He went to Moscow on May 11, 1901, and was examined by a famous consultant, who said his state had worsened and ordered him to go at once to a sanatorium in the distant province of Ufa, where patients took the koumiss cure: drinking the fermented milk of mares. The marriage took place in a Moscow church on May 25; neither his family nor Olga's friends were told or invited. There were four witnesses: Olga's uncle, and her brother, and two students. A few close friends were invited to a special luncheon, at which the bride and groom did not turn up. Chekhov and his wife went to see Olga's mother briefly, then took the train to Nizhny Novgorod to see Gorky, who had been exiled there, and after that they went by boat to Ufa and on across the steppe by coach to the sanatorium.

He sent a telegram to his mother, asking for her blessing, and saying: "Everything will remain as before."

The shock of his marriage was felt most strongly by his sister, for she had been closer to him than anyone else in his working life. Mariya ("Masha") had managed his practical affairs. Her help had been indispensable in his social doctoring and in the building of schools at Melikhovo and in the detail of organizing his complex practical fight against the cholera. She had sacrificed her chances of marriage. When she had been with Chekhov in the Ukraine they had spent some time with a landowner, Alexander Smagin, who had fallen in love with her and she with him. Smagin indeed had come to stay at Melikhovo, and she asked her brother anxiously what she should do. He stared at her for a long time and said nothing. She read the meaning of it: she broke with Smagin, and she wrote after her brother's death that he had made two people who loved each other miserably unhappy for years. Chekhov's blank stare was unanswerable. It is extraordinary to see Chekhov become as ruthless as the woman teacher who destroys the love affair of her pretty sister in *The House with the Mezzanine*.

Now, deeply hurt above all because Olga, who had been her friend, had not confided in her, Mariya struggled to master her distress. She wrote to her brother: "For me you have always been the nearest and dearest person and your happiness is my only concern." And then, overwrought, she made an extraordinary proposal: she asked to be allowed to visit the couple on their honeymoon. He replied that he and Olga would be delighted by this. Mariya, wisely, decided not to join them.

The journey to Ufa had enlivened the traveler. Everything went well, despite the primitive condition of the sanatorium. The oak woods around it were beautiful. Chekhov delighted in the wildflowers and was thrilled by the droves of wild horses and, of course, went fishing. He made an effort to drink bottle after bottle of mares' milk and his weight went up at once. Olga and he were happy, though he hated to be without books and having to depend on newspapers that were a year old. He missed, above all, the talk of his intellectual friends: Olga had noticed long ago that he rarely talked about literature to her and as an earnest, educated, half-German Russian, she felt that he believed her not to be up to it and that he evaded the subject with his usual jokes. The cure was supposed to last two months, but at the end of a month he decided to go back with Olga to his house in Yalta, where his mother and sister were, as usual, staying for the summer. For the women the situation was difficult. Who had the natural right to rule, the wife or the sister? In the past Masha had taken charge of looking after Chekhov's diet and health, had seen that he washed his hair and brushed his clothes and that he changed his ties. Although Masha's jealousy of her friend had faded, it revived when she heard Olga say she was thinking of giving up the theater and becoming a teacher in order to look after her husband.

Before the marriage Chekhov had made his will. Masha was to have his house "during her lifetime and the income from my dramatic productions." To his wife he left one of his Crimean cottages. Decent sums were left to his brothers. After his mother's and Masha's deaths what remained, except the income from the plays, was to go to the Taganrog administration for public education. He clearly felt that the young Olga would be in far less need because of her now successful career.

Olga returned to Moscow, and he was soon bored and longing for her. He joined her briefly to see a performance of *The Seagull* in its new season and was at last delighted by it. They saw very little of each other because her rehearsals went on for hours, even into the night. She loved late parties, she could sing well, was a good pianist and, naturally, a good linguist, and she did not hide her excitement at being the wife of "the Russian Maupassant." But he could not keep up with her energetic life in Moscow. He and Masha would wait for her to return, often after midnight, from rehearsals or sprees, in the new large flat he and Olga had taken. Not surprisingly Chekhov's illness returned and he had to go back to Yalta once more alone, but it was clear that his sister had now accepted the situation and, although still watchful, was calmer.

The story of Chekhov's happy marriage to Olga is plain in the letters they wrote almost every day in their absences. Then in June 1902 comes their tragedy. She is pregnant, at first without knowing it; then she tells him and he is full of joy. They talk about their "little half German." He longs for a son and he tries to stop her going to all those exciting parties that last half the night. He has heard of them from her but also from his worried sister. Olga miscarries: her hope of having a "little half German" has gone.

For a time Olga talks of giving up the theater so that they can spend all their time together, but Chekhov will not hear of it. It occurs to her that he says this because he would be bored in her continuous company. She has a sudden attack of peritonitis and Chekhov is patiently nursing her in a villa outside Moscow.

When he saw she was recovering he abruptly went off on a long journey to Perm with a millionaire mill-owner, Morozov, who regarded himself as a revolutionary of sorts. Olga was hurt that he did not invite her to join them. The journey was not the last fling of the restless nomad.

Chapter Seventeen

The young novelist Bunin had long talks with Chekhov at Yalta and later wrote the best portrait we have of him in these last years. He saw the wasted body, the strangely darkened face, and noticed how, when he took off his pince-nez, he looked younger. He noticed how he lisped on some syllables when he talked and how he would suddenly flash with excitement, but more often spoke tonelessly, yet said the most bizarre things without a smile and loved a fantastic image. (He spoke of a boring, nonstop talker who was Tolstoy's emissary, as being like "a funeral cart standing up on end.") One evening Chekhov was walking with Bunin to his lodgings up a dark street and he saw a lighted window and said: "Did you hear that Bunin had been murdered there by a Tatar?" Another time Chekhov spoke of his own death and said that in seven years he would be forgotten and that people would say, "A good writer, but not as good as Turgenev," a line that came from Trigorin in *The Seagull*.

At this period he was working on two stories: one, *The Bishop*, is one of his finest works and reads like a sustained anthem to his own death. The other is *The Bride,* sometimes called *The Betrothed* or *The Fiancée*. These are his last stories, written while he was working on his two great plays *The Three Sisters* and *The Cherry Orchard*. *The Bishop* returns to his early manner in *The Artist* and *The Student*, to his delight in the chants and ceremonies of the Orthodox Church, his love of the naïveté of its deacons, the drollery of the "chaff and grain" in their pious lives.

The bishop, like Chekhov, has risen to fame from humble peasant origins, and at the end of his life he finds he is no longer regarded as an ordinary human being. The awe he inspires leaves him isolated: fame and rank have turned him into an institution. Now he is concerned with the rediscovery of his human self. There is something dreamlike yet totally exact in the marvelous opening pages, something plain yet melodiously Proustian in the glide from the particular to its associations. We see the bishop standing near the altar on the Eve of Palm Sunday, looking at a vast congregation:

When they began distributing the palm it was close upon ten o'clock, the candles were burning dimly, the wicks wanted snuffing; it was all in a sort of mist. In the twilight of the church the crowd seemed heaving like the sea, and to Bishop Pyotr, who had been unwell for the last three days, it seemed that all the faces—old and young, men's and women's—were alike, that everyone who came up for the palm had the same expression in his eyes. In the mist he could not see the doors [of the cathedral]; the crowd kept moving and looked as though there were no end to it. The female choir was singing, a nun was reading the prayers for the day. How stifling, how hot it was!

Then he is disturbed when a religious maniac utters shrieks in the gallery, and we get our first sight of his private drama:

[A]s though in a dream or delirium, it seemed to the bishop as though his own mother, . . . whom he had not seen for nine years, or some old woman just like his mother, came up to him out of the crowd, and, after taking a palm branch from him, walked away looking at him all the while good-humouredly with a kind, joyful smile until she was lost in the crowd. . . . tears flowed down his face.

And then:

Someone close at hand was weeping, then someone else farther away, then others and still others, and then little by little the church was filled with soft weeping. And a little later, within five minutes, the nuns' choir was singing; and no one was weeping and everything was as before.

After the service the bishop drives off in his carriage and we hear the changing sound of the horses' hooves as they strike the sandy road. In the moonlight "the white walls, the white crosses on the tombs, the white birch-trees and black shadows, and the far-away moon in the sky exactly over the convent, seemed now living their own life, apart and incomprehensible, yet very near to man." In the town an enterprising shopkeeper has just put in electric lighting, a wonder that attracts the crowd. Suddenly we find that Chekhov has played one of his dramatic tricks: the bishop arrives at his rooms at the monastery and finds that the woman who had smiled at him in the church was indeed his mother, a woman who had had nine children and forty grandchildren and who had suddenly taken it into her head to make the long journey from her village just for the sight of her famous son. We are at the heart of the drama: the relationship of a simple peasant mother with a famous son who has moved into a position of learning, power and sacredness, who has even been on foreign missions. She brings a naughty little niece with her and later we shall see the unawed child showing off and knocking a glass off the table where they are eating. (Amusing, but Chekhov is aware of the comic principle that accidents must happen twice and, later, to advance the story, the child knocks a saucer over before the meal is done.) The naughty child tells the bishop that his stomach is making a noise, and that his cousin Nikolay, a medical student, "cuts up dead people." She is behaving badly with a purpose. Her father had died because he had a bad throat. Her chin begins quivering. She puts on the manner of a little peasant beggar and makes tears come to her eyes:

"Your holiness," she said in a shrill voice . . . "uncle, mother and all of us are left very wretched. . . . Give us a little money, do be kind, Uncle darling."

Suddenly after this meal the bishop is ill. Perhaps the fish he has eaten at dinner is the cause? He notices that his legs are numb and he cannot understand what he is standing on. At night he cannot sleep, for Sisoy, a rough servant-monk who is in the cell next door, mutters and snores loudly without a break. The bishop's mind wanders over trivial incidents of his early years in his village, remembering priests who got drunk and saw green snakes, and the nephew of the priest whose task, at services, was to read out the names of the parishioners who were ill and who needed prayers for their souls. Memories of childhood and youth come back, "living, fair and joyful as in all likelihood it never had been." Perhaps in the life to come, he thinks, we shall remember our "distant past, our life here, with the same feeling. Who knows?" In the morning he is roughly woken by Sisoy. From church to convent in his district the bishop travels throughout Holy Week, seeing supplicants, and on his return has to meet visitors. It irks him to hear his mother, who does not know how to talk to him, chattering away easily to Sisoy and others about goodness knows what, except that in every story she always begins with the words "Having had tea," or "Having drunk tea," as if she had done nothing but drink tea all her life.

Now the bishop is very ill. He has got typhoid, Sisoy tells him brutally, and the monk insists on rubbing his body with tallow. Doctors are called and the bishop knows for certain that he is dying.

"How good," he thought. He has attained what he has longed for: "Insignificance."

His simple mother sits with him and she has forgotten

he is a bishop and now calls him "my darling son" and says, "Why are you like this? Answer."

The night before Easter Sunday he is dead.

What happens in a little town like this one when a famous man dies? Nothing. On the morning of Easter Sunday, as always, the joyful bells clang, the birds sing, the spring air quivers; in the market square barrel organs play, the accordions are squeaking, the drunks are shouting. After midday people began driving in carriages up and down.

Notice the precision of that return to the normal habits of the town. Notice also that at the end of the story Chekhov returns to his inner theme. Like an ordinary person, the bishop is forgotten. Except by his mother,

who is living today with her son-in-law the deacon in a remote little district town, [and] when she goes out at night to bring her cow in and meets other women at the pasture, [she] begins talking of her children, her grandchildren, and says that she had a son a bishop, and this she says timidly, afraid that she may not be believed. And, indeed, there are some who do not believe her.

Chapter Eighteen

As we have seen, Chekhov draws on his short stories for the important characters and themes of his plays. In the stories his people live under the directing authority of his prose and are not at the mercy of producer or actors—a matter which plagued him; he had his own strict interpretation of the difference between the tragic and the dramatic. He was always angered when he was defined as a master of "twilight moods."

If we turn to Donald Rayfield's excellent work *Chekhov: The Evolution of His Art*, we find he says something decisive on Chekhov's last plays and especially on *The Three Sisters*, the longest and greatest of them. Rayfield notes that the total effect is symphonic; the play moves as a symphony does from movement to movement as it gathers power. The theme of changing time is set at once by the striking of a clock that interrupts the chatter of the three sisters on a happy May morning. Olga, the eldest, who is twenty-eight, remembers:

It is exactly a year ago today since Father died—on the fifth of May, your name-day, Irina. It was very cold then and snowing . . . but now a year has gone by and we don't mind talking about it. You are wearing your white dress again and you look radiant. . . . The clock struck twelve then too. I remember the band playing when they took Father to the cemetery and they fired a salute. He was a general and commanded a Brigade. All the same, not many people came.

That last flat sentence tells us something of importance about the isolation of the family. The girls are trapped in a dull provincial town, alien to their cultivated upbringing. They long to get back to the wonderful earlier life they had in Moscow. Their longing is revived by the arrival of a new artillery brigade in the town. Two or three of the officers have known the girls and their family in Moscow when the girls were young; the soldiers seem to be messengers of release.

Chekhov had turned to an early story, *The Kiss*, written when he was at Babkino and studied an artillery brigade stationed there, a story that has something of Tolstoy's understanding of the ethos of military life. Chekhov understood that a regiment is a disciplined and migrant culture passing through a stationary society. He also understood that since the officers were under orders, they became uprooted and solitary daydreamers on their monotonous journeys, and that this gave them a bond with the daydreaming sisters. In their isolation the simple officers become amateur philosophers. They brood on large insoluble questions, their private longings and sentimentalities. Disciplined, they see undisciplined Russia: they speculate about the "good life." Vershinin, the decent middle-aged commanding officer, has his private miseries: he is the victim of an unlucky marriage to a wife who is a suicidal neurotic, and who joins him at his postings. Messages come that his wife has once more taken poison and he has to drop everything to go and protect his children. (He could very well have been the young officer in *The Kiss* who was stamped for life by his failure to trace the girl who kissed him in the dark, and who became obsessed by his failure.) Tuzenbakh is a stolid baron who believes, in his simplicity, that manual labor is the solution to Russian evils! He dreams of leaving the army and establishing brickfields—a life that will appeal to the idealism of the youngest sister, Irina. His enemy is a pestering Captain Solyony, a querulous and jealous adolescent who has failed to grow up and has dreams of becoming a romantic Byronic figure like the duelist in Lermontov's *A Hero of Our Time*. He is looking for someone to fight. There is the old idle army doctor Chebutykin, a cynic who likes to fancy he had been the lover of the sisters' mother in Moscow. Life is meaningless, he believes; he drinks too much, reads out stupid items from the papers and occasionally sings out lines from a silly song—"Tararaboomdeay." There are parties, dances, flirtations; love affairs begin. Even Masha, who reads Pushkin aloud and who is married to a boring foolish schoolmaster from the town, will have a secret love affair with the worried Vershinin before the play is done.

The sisters do not realize that the wrecker of their future

is their brother, Andrey. He has easily given up the ambitions of his Moscow days—he had intended to be a professor—and has sunk to a minor job on the town council and to gambling at cards in this provincial backwater. He has fallen in love with Natasha, a shrewd local girl, one of Chekhov's predatory women, and has married her. She becomes, by this marriage, the ruler of the house, and her provincial manners are mocked by the sisters. She is an ambitious secretive schemer. She has become the mistress of the powerful chairman of the town council, who does not appear in the play. Her only weakness is her ridiculous, if cunning, fuss about her baby. We soon hear whispers that the brother has gambled away his sisters' inheritance.

It was Chekhov's rule that a play must come to a decisive head in the third act. There is a sudden fire in the town—two streets of wooden houses are burned to the ground—and the soldiers help to fight it. We know of the fire by the sound of the galloping horses of the fire brigade, also by the reflected red glow on the walls of the room in which the sisters, overwrought by taking in refugees, are exchanging confidences. They are interrupted in their confessions and are scared by the sight of Natasha, asserting her power by crossing the room where they are huddled, carrying a lighted candle and ignoring them. It is the most arresting moment in the play. She is Lady Macbeth reborn. Masha says: "She goes about looking as if she started the fire." Yes, Natasha is the spirit of destruction. We have already seen her cruelty when she sacks the eighty-year-old servant who has worked for the family all her life. Andrey, too, has seen his wife's imperious "walk." Confused by his guilt about what he has done to his sisters, he protests that he loves his wife and that they are wrong to hate her. She is splendid, he says, and they must stop hating her. Suddenly he shouts: "Don't believe a word of what I've said." He confesses he has mortgaged the property to pay his debts.

In the last act the play is haunted not simply by the good-byes of the soldiers and the girls as the army prepares to move off. The partings begin. We shall see Masha's guilt as she says good-bye to Vershinin. Her decent ridiculous husband, the schoolmaster, puts on a false beard and mustache he has taken from a boy in his class and clowns to prevent Masha from confessing her guilt. The fool loves her and she is grateful. But laughter and tears are not enough. Theater requires horror. Everyone half knows that the baron and the jealous Solyony are absent for no good reason. There is the sound of a shout from across the fields. It is not a shout but a shot: Solyony has had his duel and killed the baron. Chebutykin, the believer in meaninglessness, reacts to this tragedy with a typical display of indifference. He takes a newspaper out of his pocket and sings his familiar silly song: "Tararaboomdeay." The collector of *faits divers* from the newspapers is enjoying being adjacent to catastrophe. Why? No reason at all except that it supports his doctrine: "Nothing matters." God has become the Absurd, or, rather, the Indifferent.

At the house Natasha, the vulgar interloper, says that she intends to have their lovely avenue of firs cut down "because it looks awful in the evenings." She is going to have a proper little suburban avenue of garden flowers. She sees a maid has left a table fork on a chair and screams at the maid:

"Don't answer me back"—the voice of power and pettiness made absolute.

Farewells are over. We see the sisters listening to the distant, stirring, mocking sound of the army band as the soldiers march away. The symphony is over. Olga comforts Masha. As she weeps Irina cries, "Why do we have to suffer so much?" but clings to Chekhov's remedy: we must work and work and think of nothing else. The most searing line comes from Olga: "In time we shall pass on for ever and be forgotten. Our faces will be forgotten and our voices, and [most piercingly of all] no one will even know how many of us there were."

What has moved us so much? As in real life the feeling lies not in the words that are said, but in what lies unspoken between the words. Even the abused *things* of this household play their part.

Before turning to his last play, Chekhov turned to what would be his last story. It exists in five versions and is *The Bride*. Many Russian and English critics have seen it as being "more affirmative" or "positive" than the rest of his later writing because the heroine, Nadya, breaks with her provincial family and leaves her home to go to Petersburg to be reeducated. She is stirred by the wild talk of Sasha, a young painter, who talks about "the glorious future." He is obviously dying of consumption and she has been captivated by what she supposes is his genius. In fact he has failed as a painter and is no more than a lithographer in a modest printing works. His stirring speeches are those of a man recklessly deceiving himself but she has learned something from him: one must rebel. Sasha has at least made her break with the pompous conventional son of a priest to whom she was engaged. There is a remarkable scene in which her fiancé takes her to inspect the house and conventional pictures and furnishings which would be her future home. No elation there! What a prison! Her future husband's only gift is the absurd squeaking and grunting preoccupation with playing the violin. There is a wonderful moment when Chekhov uses his old trick with sounds: one day a string snaps.

In a letter to Olga Chekhov said he was writing this story in the "style of the seventies," which suggests his study of self-satisfied bourgeois life in *Three Years*. He said he was writing slowly, a spoonful at a time—"possibly because there are a lot of characters or because I've lost the knack." Not quite, for in a few lines he establishes the dead town. One quiet evening Nadya stands listening to the distant croaking of the frogs, which makes the place seem "much larger than it really is." Chekhov evokes the finicking house-proud mother and her pride in her jewelry. We hear Sasha's denunciation of the beetle- and bug-infested kitchens where the servants sleep on the floor. Much of Sasha's talk will recall Trofimov's outburst in *The Cherry Orchard*. There is a savage moment when the prim garden of the house is slashed by the autumn winds. News comes that Sasha, who has been taking the koumiss cure, has died, and Nadya leaves home for good. The last words of this story are enigmatic:

In a lively, cheerful mood she left the town, forever, as she thought.

Her rebellion is positive. There are no tears. She will, as Sasha has urged her, "educate herself." Many critics have thought that in the portrait of the dying Sasha Chekhov is in some degree mocking himself.

The importance of the story really lies in details that connect it with the writing of *The Cherry Orchard*.

Chapter Nineteen

Chekhov started writing *The Cherry Orchard* in Yalta in February 1903. He wrote to Olga, who was in Moscow and whom he called his "little pony," that a crowd of characters was gathering in his mind but he could only manage to write four lines a day and "even that gives me intolerable pain." His disease was possessing his whole body, moving to his intestines and his bowels. Olga came to Yalta in July, hoping the play would be finished in time for her to take a fair copy back to Moscow in September when the theater season opened. It was not ready because he was continuously revising what he had written, but also because, in his anxiety about money, he had agreed to become the literary editor of a new magazine which had been started by his liberal admirer Lavrov, and he was reading dozens of manuscripts for him. At last the play was finished, "except for difficulties with the second act." Stanislavsky and Nemirovich-Danchenko sent him long and enthusiastic telegrams. There was only one jarring note: Stanislavsky had called the play "a truly great tragedy." Tartly, and fearing Stanislavsky's possessiveness, Chekhov replied that it was not even a drama—"It is a farce."

The central subject of *The Cherry Orchard* seems to have been taken from Chekhov's story *A Visit to Friends*, written in 1898, which deals with the bankruptcy of the Kiselev family, with whom he had stayed many times at Babkino. Chekhov did not include the story in the complete edition of his work and it has been suggested that he did not want to offend the family: but the story may very well have been rejected because it is too labored in a novelizing way. In the story, the family have turned cynically to a shrewd and successful young lawyer, hoping against hope that he will find some way of saving them from ruin: he knows so many rich people. The wife thinks the solution lies in getting him to marry their daughter. He *is* sentimentally attracted to her, but self-interest is stronger than sentiment: he simply sneaks away in the night. The young man is ashamed of his behavior.

In *The Cherry Orchard,* Lopakhin, the property speculator, evades all appeals to marry Ranevskaya's ward. He seems to be a new version of the shrewd plain practical railway engineer who appears in *Lights* and more fully in the excellent *My Life*, a man with a businesslike eye for taking over the properties of the feckless landowning families. Chekhov admired this self-made man and he warned Stanislavsky that Lopakhin must not be played as a greedy vulgarian; he saw that Lopakhin's weakness was that he would be too cautious and inhibited in love. Ranevskaya must not be played as an entirely frivolous and irresponsible spendthrift: she is all heart; her sensuality is natural to her and not vicious. In her reckless life in Paris she has nursed a lover who has deceived and robbed her, and she will return to him at the end of the play when he is ill again and appeals to her once more. She is shrewd when she mocks Trofimov, the high-minded and self-absorbed "eternal student" who has been the family tutor, because, at his age, he has never had a mistress. He is, she says, a prig. She may be a victim of what Chekhov called *morbus fraudulentus* when she gazes at her cherry orchard and sees in the white blossoms the symbol of the lost innocence of her girlhood, but the incurable lavishness of her heart is genuine. Lopakhin will not forget the moment she tenderly washed his face when his nose was bleeding when he was a little boy, and called him "little peasant." In Lopakhin, the tongue-tied money-maker, that childhood memory is a genuine grace. What Chekhov brings out, as he makes his people tell their own story without listening to one another, is their absurd pride in their own history and their indifference to everyone else's. Ranevskaya may long for the tongue-tied Lopakhin to propose to her ward, but the girl's real dream is for a life of pious journeys from convent to convent.

The truly desperate character is the bizarre half-German outsider, Sharlotta, who breaks the tension of the play by her mystifying tricks with cards and her ventriloquism. Chekhov had seen such a girl at a fair on one of his trips. She is the daughter of anarchy and is truly frightening. Everyone else knows who they are. She does not know who she is. "I have no proper identity papers and I don't know how old I am. I keep imagining I am young. . . . Where I come from and who I am I do not know." All she knows is that she has traveled, when she was a child, from fair to fair and that her gypsy parents taught her to do card tricks. A German lady rescued her and turned her into a governess. She pulls a cucumber out of her pocket and eats it. "I am so lonely, always so lonely . . . and who I am, what I exist for, nobody knows." Pathos? Not at all—a wild independent native homelessness. In the final scene of the play, in the general good-byes when the house is sold, she picks up a bundle, pretends it is a baby, produces the illusion of a baby crying as she sings "Hush, little baby, my heart goes out to you," and then throws the bundle on the floor and says to them all: "And please find me another job. I can't go on like this."

What about the eloquent speech of Trofimov, the eternal student, sent down twice from the university, working for the "glorious future" in Russia? He attacks the theorizing intelligentsia and proudly refuses a loan from Lopakhin at the end of the play. In Act II he cries out: "The whole of Russia is our orchard." Is he a proud prophet of revolution and reform? Hardly: he is a rootless enthusiastic bookworm.

Objection has been made to the final scene, in which Firs, the sick and rambling old servant, lover of the old days, is left behind when the family leave, locked in by mistake. The family had assumed he was in the hospital and no one had troubled to find out. Is this eerie or simply anticlimax? It "works," for he is the very conscious historian of the family in a play which is notable for its pairs of matching scenes. For we remember that in the wild ballroom scene in the third act, Chekhov has brought in the local stationmaster, who insists on reciting a notorious poem called "The Sinful

Woman." It is clearly directed at Ranevskaya's adultery. He is seemingly unembarrassed by his tactlessness and may even be thinking that he is celebrating her fame in local gossip. No one listens. But it is Firs who enlarges the history of the family. He says:

> We used to have generals, barons and admirals at our dances in the old days, but now we send for the post-office clerk and the stationmaster and even they are not all that keen to come.

He rambles on about the good old days of serfdom:

> I feel frail. The old master, Mr. Leonid's grandfather, used to dose us all with powdered sealing wax no matter what was wrong with us. I've been taking powdered sealing wax for twenty years or more and maybe that is what's kept me alive.

The matching of time present and time past gives the play the density and intricacy of a novel; the play is the most novelized of Chekhov's plays because the people talk it into existence and because no one listens. It *is* a farce because the people are a disordered chorus who have lost their gods and invent themselves. They are a collective farewell, and that is what moves us. As Professor Rayfield has written, the play is also Chekhov's farewell to Russia and his genius.

There was the usual trouble, especially with Stanislavsky, but even with Nemirovich-Danchenko, when rehearsals began. The premiere was on January 17, 1904. Chekhov was too ill to go to it but he was taken, against his will, to see the end of the third act. The occasion was arranged as the celebration of his twenty-five years as a writer. Chekhov loathed celebrations and listening to speeches. A journalist wrote:

He stood in the middle of the stage, tall and haggard, stooping and fidgeting with his hands, in a short-tailed morning coat, rather short trousers, with dishevelled hair and gray beard. Someone in the gallery called out kindly, "Sit down," but there was no chair on the stage.

He was with Olga and in February she described how on a sunny day, though the frost was hard, they took a trip by train into the country and came back by sleigh; he loved the white plains gleaming in the sun and the crunch of the runners on the smooth snow. The Russo-Japanese war had started and Chekhov was planning to go to the front as a doctor in June if he felt well enough.

"What is the meaning of life?" Olga asked in a letter when he was back in Yalta. He replied: "It is like asking what a carrot is. A carrot is a carrot and nothing more is known."

In Yalta he lay in bed, emaciated, almost unrecognizable, and suffering great pain in his stomach, to which the disease had traveled. His doctor advised him to go to the German spa of Badenweiler in the Black Forest. It was plain that he would never return to Russia. This would be the nomad's last trip. Olga traveled with him to Berlin; then on they went to the spa and they stayed in a guest house. The German doctors turned him upside down, he said, but the routine of treatment was "pleasant." He was given an enormous amount of butter to eat. For a time his health improved, and by the middle of June he wrote to his sister—to whom he sent regular bulletins—that his weight was increasing, not by ounces but by pounds, and that he was able to go for walks in the sun. But Chekhov and Olga had to leave the guest house because the owners feared a death would drive away other guests. The couple moved to a cosy room at an hotel, and he would sit on the balcony watching the crowds going to the post office to collect letters. "That means everyone can read," he wrote. "When will our peasants in Russia be like that? There is more talent in Russian villages: in Germany there is no talent but there is order and honesty."

The doctor thought that Chekhov's heart was bad, but that his lungs were strong enough to last for another four to six months. Chekhov was already talking of returning to Russia by way of Trieste and Lake Como, even of joining an expedition to the Arctic! But he clearly knew he would die much earlier for he sent a check to a Berlin bank and asked for the money to be made out to his wife's name.

A few hours before he died, on July 2, 1904, Chekhov was telling Olga a story about an hotel packed with fat Englishmen and Americans who one evening discovered that the cook had left and there was no dinner. Olga was laughing at his account of how each of the guests reacted to this. A few hours later he was gasping for breath. They were going to send for oxygen but Chekhov said he would be dead before it came, so a bottle of champagne was brought. He sipped it and soon began to ramble and he evidently had one of those odd visions that he had evoked in *Ward 6*. "Has the sailor gone?" he asked. What sailor? Perhaps his sailor in *Gusev*? Then he said in Russian, "I am dying," then in German, "Ich sterbe," and died at once. Olga said his face suddenly looked very young, contented and "almost happy." Very strangely, she had not expected him to die.

The journey back to Moscow and the funeral had elements of farce that would have delighted Chekhov; Gorky was infuriated. The coffin had been put into a goods wagon labeled Fresh Oysters, and in Moscow the mourners got mixed up with another funeral, that of a General Keller of Manchuria, to the sound of a military band. Part of the small crowd mourning for Chekhov followed the wrong procession. "That is how we treat our great writers," Gorky wrote.

Chekhov was buried beside his father's grave.

Index

FOR THE BEST IN PAPERBACKS, LOOK FOR THE 🐧

In every corner of the world, on every subject under the sun, Penguin represents quality and variety – the very best in publishing today.

For complete information about books available from Penguin – including Pelicans, Puffins, Peregrines and Penguin Classics – and how to order them, write to us at the appropriate address below. Please note that for copyright reasons the selection of books varies from country to country.

In the United Kingdom: Please write to *Dept E.P., Penguin Books Ltd, Harmondsworth, Middlesex, UB7 0DA*

If you have any difficulty in obtaining a title, please send your order with the correct money, plus ten per cent for postage and packaging, to *PO Box No 11, West Drayton, Middlesex*

In the United States: Please write to *Dept BA, Penguin, 299 Murray Hill Parkway, East Rutherford, New Jersey 07073*

In Canada: Please write to *Penguin Books Canada Ltd, 2801 John Street, Markham, Ontario L3R 1B4*

In Australia: Please write to the *Marketing Department, Penguin Books Australia Ltd, P.O. Box 257, Ringwood, Victoria 3134*

In New Zealand: Please write to the *Marketing Department, Penguin Books (NZ) Ltd, Private Bag, Takapuna, Auckland 9*

In India: Please write to *Penguin Overseas Ltd, 706 Eros Apartments, 56 Nehru Place, New Delhi, 110019*

In Holland: Please write to *Penguin Books Nederland B.V., Postbus 195, NL–1380AD Weesp, Netherlands*

In Germany: Please write to *Penguin Books Ltd, Friedrichstrasse 10–12, D–6000 Frankfurt Main 1, Federal Republic of Germany*

In Spain: Please write to *Longman Penguin España, Calle San Nicolas 15, E–28013 Madrid, Spain*

In France: Please write to *Penguin Books Ltd, 39 Rue de Montmorency, F-75003, Paris, France*

In Japan: Please write to *Longman Penguin Japan Co Ltd, Yamaguchi Building, 2–12–9 Kanda Jimbocho, Chiyoda-Ku, Tokyo 101, Japan*

FOR THE BEST IN PAPERBACKS, LOOK FOR THE 🐧

PENGUIN CLASSICS

Klaus von Clausewitz	**On War**
Friedrich Engels	**The Origins of the Family, Private Property and the State**
Wolfram von Eschenbach	**Parzival**
	Willehalm
Goethe	**Elective Affinities**
	Faust
	Italian Journey 1786–88
	The Sorrows of Young Werther
Jacob and Wilhelm Grimm	**Selected Tales**
E. T. A. Hoffmann	**Tales of Hoffmann**
Henrik Ibsen	**The Doll's House/The League of Youth/The Lady from the Sea**
	Ghosts/A Public Enemy/When We Dead Wake
	Hedda Gabler/The Pillars of the Community/The Wild Duck
	The Master Builder/Rosmersholm/Little Eyolf/John Gabriel Borkman/
	Peer Gynt
Søren Kierkegaard	**Fear and Trembling**
Friedrich Nietzsche	**Beyond Good and Evil**
	Ecce Homo
	A Nietzsche Reader
	Thus Spoke Zarathustra
	Twilight of the Idols and **The Anti-Christ**
Friedrich Schiller	**The Robbers** and **Wallenstein**
Arthur Schopenhauer	**Essays and Aphorisms**
Gottfried von Strassburg	**Tristan**
August Strindberg	**Inferno** and **From an Occult Diary**

Anton Chekhov	The Duel and Other Stories
	The Kiss and Other Stories
	Lady with Lapdog and Other Stories
	Plays (The Cherry Orchard/Ivanov/The Seagull/Uncle Vanya/The Bear/The Proposal/A Jubilee/Three Sisters
	The Party and Other Stories
Fyodor Dostoyevsky	The Brothers Karamazov
	Crime and Punishment
	The Devils
	The Gambler/Bobok/A Nasty Story
	The House of the Dead
	The Idiot
	Netochka Nezvanova
	Notes From Underground and The Double
Nikolai Gogol	Dead Souls
	Diary of a Madman and Other Stories
Maxim Gorky	My Apprenticeship
	My Childhood
	My Universities
Mikhail Lermontov	A Hero of Our Time
Alexander Pushkin	Eugene Onegin
	The Queen of Spades and Other Stories
Leo Tolstoy	Anna Karenin
	Childhood/Boyhood/Youth
	The Cossacks/The Death of Ivan Ilyich/Happy Ever After
	The Kreutzer Sonata and Other Stories
	Master and Man and Other Stories
	Resurrection
	The Sebastopol Sketches
	War and Peace
Ivan Turgenev	Fathers and Sons
	First Love
	Home of the Gentry
	A Month in the Country
	On the Eve
	Rudin

Tolstoy *A. N. Wilson*

'One of the best biographies of our century' – Leon Edel

'Masterly . . . it is his best book by far . . . All his skills as a writer, his fire as a critic, his insight as a novelist and his experience of life, have come together in this subject . . . he makes the life and works clarify and empower one another. He misses nothing' – Peter Levi in the *Independent*

'This is an extraordinary biography, and I warmly recommend it . . . Wilson is splendid. He is an acute literary critic, with a novelist's insight. He has a deep and discriminating love of Tolstoy's writings, and a lively curiosity about the relations between the writings and the peculiarities of the life . . . full of sharp and startling perceptions' – Conor Cruise O'Brien in the *Sunday Times*

'Immense in scope, acute in its judgements, it sustains with an engaged intimacy of tone its wonderful readability to the end' – Michael Holroyd